the
words we
pray

Other books by Amy Welborn

Loyola Kids Book of Saints

Loyola Kids Book of Heroes

Six Weeks with the Bible: Parables: Stories of the Kingdom

Six Weeks with the Bible: Matthew 26–28: Jesus' Life-Giving
    Death

the
words we
pray

Discovering the Richness
of Traditional Catholic Prayers

Amy Welborn

LOYOLAPRESS.

CHICAGO

LOYOLAPRESS.

3441 N. ASHLAND AVENUE
CHICAGO, ILLINOIS 60657
(800) 621-1008
WWW.LOYOLABOOKS.ORG

Scripture excerpts are taken from the *New American Bible with Revised New Testament and Revised Psalms,* copyright © 1991, 1986, 1970 by the Confraternity of Christian Doctrine, Washington, D.C. Used with permission. All rights reserved. No part of the *New American Bible* may be reproduced by any means without permission in writing from the copyright owner.

Sign of the Cross, Our Father, Hail Mary, Prayers before and after meals and Guardian Angel prayer are in public domain.

English translation of the Apostles' Creed, Glory to the Father, Benedictus and the Nicene Creed by the International Consultation on English Texts.

The English translation of the Memorare is from *A Book of Prayers* © 1982, International Committee on English in the Liturgy, Inc. All rights reserved.

The Morning Offering from the Web site of the U.S. office of The Apostleship of Prayer.
http://www.apostlesofprayer.org/Daily%20Offering.htm

Hail Holy Queen and Prayer to St. Michael from *The Complete Catholic Handbook* (Britons Catholic Library), p. 67 and 78.

The Act of Contrition, The Prayer before Meals, and The Prayer after Meals are from the *Catholic Source Book* (Orlando: Brown-ROA, 2000), p. 8.

The Jesus Prayer is from Lev Gillet, *The Jesus Prayer,* (Crestwood, N. Y.: St. Vladimir's Seminary Press, 1987), p. 69.

Anima Christi and Suscipe are from *The Spiritual Exercises of St. Ignatius of Loyola,* trans. Louis J. Puhl, S.J. (Chicago: Loyola University Press, 1951).

Peace Prayer of St. Francis from "A Prayer in Search of an Author" in *Greyfriars Review,* vol. 10, no. 5. p. 257.

Canticle of the Sun from Regis J. Armstrong, O.F.M. CAP. and Ignatius C. Brady, O.F.M., eds., *Francis and Clare: The Complete Works* (New York: Paulist Press, 1982) 38, 39.

Veni Creator Spiritus is traditional. This version is found at http://home.earthlink.net/˜thesaurus/thesaurus/Hymni/VeniCreator.html.

Cover image by John Turner, Turner/Getty Images

Caver and interior design by Arc Group Ltd.

Library of Congress Cataloging-in-Publication Data

Welborn, Amy.
   The words we pray : discovering the richness of traditional Catholic prayers / Amy Welborn
      p. cm.
   Includes bibliographical references.
   ISBN 0-8294-1956-X
   1. Catholic Church—Prayer-books and devotions—English—History and criticism. I. Title.
BX2130.W45 2004
242'.802—dc22

                                                                    2004011117

Printed in the United States of America
06 07 08 09 10 Bang 10 9 8 7 6 5 4 3

To Michael
Sirach 7:14–15

Contents

The Journey from "You've Got a Friend" to Salve Regina

It was the 1970s, and I was a student in a Catholic high school, so of course I learned to pray.

I learned how to meditate on flickering candle flames, a budding flower in a vase, and the ceiling tiles. I was guided in contemplation of songs by James Taylor, Simon and Garfunkel, and Bread, and if it was a "really good" prayer experience, I cried.

Although I shake my head over it now, I can see how all of that practice took me to a point in my senior year when, on our class retreat with Jesuits in Atlanta, I could immerse myself in a bit of *lectio divina* centered on John's Passion account, be in the presence of the Presence, and give myself over to what I finally knew was real.

I still remember that encounter, and in a way I still feel the effects of it. So if contemplating (and crying to) "You've Got a Friend" helped get me there, it was good. But the bad part was that such experiences made me a bit of a prayer snob. The message I absorbed and lived with for a good long time was that the only real prayer was mental prayer–that very personal and subjective experience that was mine alone–and that anything else, especially if it involved praying with words that someone else had written, was definitely not worth my time. Only children repeated memorized prayers and then closed their eyes to go to sleep. It was what the less enlightened did for penance– repeated their memorized prayers and assumed they were taken care of. Rote recitation of prayers written by dead people was not the practice of a spiritually mature person.

Then, when I was about thirty years old, a friend made the most interesting suggestion. He thought we might pray the rosary together.

The rosary. Well, at least I owned one, with beads made of light-blue glass, most of them lightly scuffed with age and, yes, with even a bit of use (as a teen, I had fingered them often and murmured prayers to help me get to sleep).

But since then, the rosary had not been my chosen means of prayer. In fact, I hadn't practiced any prayer that I hadn't dreamed up myself in years. I did go to Mass and pray the liturgical prayers, but I probably thought that, if given a chance, I could improve on them as well.

So this is the attitude I brought to the table when my friend invited me to share in his rosary praying. But for some reason, despite my doubts, I agreed. If nothing else, the words could help me move to the really important thing, which was meditation. The words I was praying weren't nearly as important as

the state they put me in. They didn't "come from my heart."
I wasn't expressing my innermost thoughts in my own words.
But one day, months down the line, months during which the
rosary began to sink into my soul, I visited a monastery for a
weekend of retreat.

As night fell, I sat in the back of the monastery chapel,
struggling to follow along as the monks prayed Compline, the
final prayer of the day. These were difficult, transitional times
for me and for my family, and we were all at the moment deep
in a sea of disappointment and anger.

And then, as Compline drew to a close and night settled, the
monks started singing.

Hail, holy Queen, Mother of mercy

It was what all monks sing at the end of Compline, everywhere. The Salve Regina. I had never heard it before in my life.

Hail, our life, our sweetness and our hope.

The chant drifted through the chapel, settling around us like
stars emerging from the night sky.

To thee do we cry, Poor banished children of Eve

Yes. I cry, banished, my own shortsightedness and failure
bringing tears to the lives of others. What could I do?

To thee do we send up our sighs, Mourning and weeping
In this valley of tears.

All of us. My babies. My disappointed parents. Me.

Turn then, most gracious advocate, Thine eyes of mercy towards us,
Please.

O clement, O loving, O sweet Virgin Mary!

The monks raised their voices in hope at the end of each phrase, and then paused a great pause in between, letting the hope rise and then settle back into their hearts. My own heart rushed, unbidden by me, uncontrolled, right into those pauses and joined the prayer. A prayer written by an eleventh-century bedridden brother, chanted by monks in the middle of Georgia, and joined by me and the silent folk scattered in the pews around me, each with his or her own reasons to beg the Virgin for her prayers.

And we weren't the only ones joined in that prayer. With us was a great throng of other Christians who had prayed it over the centuries, and who are praying it at this very moment.

My days as a prayer snob were over.

When Our Own Words Aren't Enough

All the great saints tell us the same thing about prayer. In the end, it is nothing but being present to the God who loves us and never leaves us. St. Teresa of Ávila, the great sixteenth-century mystic and reformer of Carmelite religious life, wrote about the simplicity of prayer. She said that prayer "means taking time frequently conversing in secret with Him Who, we know, loves us."[1]

Centuries later, another Carmelite, St. Thérèse of Lisieux, took an equally uncomplicated view of prayer. She suggested that prayer is "a surge of the heart; it is a simple look turned toward heaven."[2]

God is our most intimate friend, our most faithful lover. He knows us better than we know ourselves, and he wants us to know and love him.

As with any friendship, there's simply no way to make that happen without communication, without presence. I can swear up and down that I'm you're friend, but if I never call you or spend time with you, my words are empty, and my claims to great friendship are at best a figment of my imagination, at worst a lie.

So developing that friendship with God takes communication, as the saints and common sense tells us. But how do we do that?

Bookstore shelves are filled with guides to prayer, and perhaps you've read some of them. Most of them emphasize mental prayer—meditation and contemplation—which makes sense. When people think of a deeper level of prayer, the type of prayer that might require study and practice, meditation is what they think of.

But in the midst of all of our silence, is there still room for spoken, traditional prayer? If so, where does it fit? And why should we even bother with words written by people who lived in other times and places and whose concerns and ways of thinking were different from ours? Isn't it more authentic to pray with our own words rather than depend on the words of others?

The most important quality of any prayer is that it come from the heart and that it be honest. We don't pray to prove anything or to manipulate God into seeing things our way. We pray in order to draw closer to God, and we can't do that unless we're honest. So yes, mental prayer that is rooted in our own thoughts is a vital part of that communication.

But are there times when our own words aren't enough?

Think about the times when you've had to struggle to express yourself to another person. Maybe it was when you were fifteen, deeply in love, and you were too petrified to express your feelings to the beloved. So you made a tape of a song that somehow, miraculously, put your feelings into words, with a good beat besides. What you couldn't say, the song would.

Perhaps there was a moment when reconciliation was in order, and either pride or helplessness left you speechless. What did you do? Maybe you found a poem that said it for you, or even a card that you could slip into your husband's briefcase before he left for work.

My mother was an expert at this sort of thing, at using the finely wrought words of others to make her own point. Every birthday, she sent out cards to me or her grandchildren, cards that might be unremarkable on the outside, but which on the inside she had copied, from one of her many reference books and anthologies, a most appropriate poem, all the more surprising because it was probably penned by some obscure eighteenth-century British poet. But somehow it always fit; it always captured who we were and, more important, who we could become.

We might try looking at these traditional prayers in the same way. St. Paul says that we "do not pray as we ought" (Romans 8:26). He helps us see that in the face of the complexity of life, of our great yearning, and of the mystery of

God, it can be almost impossible to come up with the words that capture the depth of our feelings, especially when we are distracted by grief or fear.

At those times, it helps to have someone else's words in front of us, words from the psalmist or one of the saints that express our need in a way that requires no more of us than we can give during a difficult time.

We're Part of Something Bigger

The words of our traditional prayers are also gifts from the past, connecting us to something very important: the entirety of the Body of Christ, as it was then, as it is now, and as it will be to come.

How many billions of times have Christians recited the Lord's Prayer? How many lips, both Jewish and Christian, have murmured the ancient words of the Psalms?

There is a sense in which each of us is alone in the universe. At the end, there is no one but us and God. We are beholden to no one but him, and he is the one we face with an accounting of how we have used this gift called life.

But we are not alone. We have billions of brothers and sisters, all of whom breathe the same air and whose souls look to the same heights for meaning and purpose.

We whisper the words of the Hail Mary at our child's bedside, in concert, in God's time, with every other mother who has looked to the Virgin for help and prayers when the burdens of parenthood seemed unbearably heavy.

Every child stumbling through the words of the Lord's Prayer, offering up simple prayers for simple needs out of the simplest, deepest love—every one of those children has countless companions lisping through the same pleas, and we are among those companions.

Together we beg God for mercy, we rage at God in confusion, we praise God in full throat. And when we do so using the Psalms, we are one with the Jews and Christians who have begged, raged, and praised for three thousand years.

We're not alone. And when we pray these ancient prayers, in the company of the living and the dead, we know this.

There's one more reason to claim these prayers as our own, another dimension of Paul's acknowledgment of our helplessness in prayer. So much of the time, we don't know what we really want.

Oh, we think we do. We sit down to pray, to present our lives to God, and we think we know exactly what we need; we're approaching God, open to his wisdom and grace and power—but on our terms.

We can't see the big picture. Understandably enough, we want our suffering to end now. We want life to change so that we're more comfortable living it.

We're like children who blame our unhappiness on the fact that it's Wednesday in the middle of math class instead of Saturday, or that we have an unappetizing plate of turnips (is there any other kind?) in front of us, or that our parents are hopeless dweebs.

We blame our inner discord on what's outside, never thinking for a moment that there might be a bigger purpose to it all, lessons to be learned, and strength to be gained.

And how often do even our circular, self-referential prayers reflect that shortsightedness? How often does our undisciplined mental prayer end up being one more kvetch, one more plea for God to change life so that we don't have to?

Here is what these ancient prayers, worn and prayed by billions, bring to that experience: They bring a sense of a wider context. They reflect the experience of the ages, the experience of those who have not only been in the mess we're in but endured to the other side of it and seen its purpose. These prayers express the wisdom of the saints, whose sharp vision helped them see God's purpose in everything both beautiful and wretched. They bring God's word, in which everything is said, if we only listen.

These prayers—conceived in the womb of God's people, brought to birth, and nurtured by their experiences of hope and faith—are treasures worth rediscovering. They give us words when words are beyond us. They link us to our brothers and sisters, past, present, and future. And they put our yearnings and questions in a context in which they will be answered by the wisdom of the holy ones and the revelatory word of God rather than kept in the confines of the present moment. When we explore the history of how these prayers were composed and used, we hook into those original impulses that gave birth to the words and shaped them, impulses and yearnings that we still possess because God is still God and we are still human. Some things have changed, but the most important things haven't.

That night in the monastery, it was hope I was looking for. Hope that God still loved me. Hope that my children would be all right. Hope that good could come out of the whole blasted mess.

I could have sat there for hours, by myself in silence, wondering, alone. But, thanks be to God, I didn't have to. In the prayers written centuries ago and kept alive by my fellow Christians over those same centuries, I found a different kind of path to mental prayer, which means, when you get down to it, another way to collapse the wall and just be more fully present to God. On this path made of well-worn and polished words, I found a way to hope that was true to my own experience and yet took me beyond it, beyond my own vision of what was wrong, to share in God's vision of what was right.

the
sign of the
cross

In the name of the Father, and of the Son, and of
the Holy Spirit.

The Holiest of All Signs

When they were baptized, none of my four children were particularly bothered by being splashed by or immersed in water. What got them was the succession of fingers messing with their foreheads.

Before the actual baptism, the presider traces a small cross on the baby's forehead as a sign of being claimed for Christ by his church. Then the presider invites parents, godparents, and—if the group is small or the priest has a lot of time on his hands—everyone in sight to do the same.

You wouldn't think that this brush of skin against skin would have such an effect, but it did. You wouldn't think a little cross would bring tears and struggle, but it did, once or twice even necessitating a liturgical intermission of sorts.

This sign of the cross marks us at the beginning of life, and as the same sign of the cross is made over our caskets, it will send us on our way at the end of life. In between, we will mark our own bodies and bow our heads as others trace the cross in the air over us thousands of times.

We can think and speak of our Christianity, but in this physical sign, this movement, our identity as Christians takes on physical form. It is a public expression, made again and again, of our faith in Christ crucified. With it we identify, we bless, and are blessed, even if at times we still resist, lest it get too close and change us.

The making of the sign of the cross is so short and so much a part of us that we hardly think of it as a prayer at all. It's more of an introduction to prayer, something to get us in the mood, a little something to get us started like "The Star-Spangled Banner" before a football game.

But it is a prayer, and while its gesture and fifteen words seem simple, the sign of the cross has a fascinating and complex history. Its contemporary usage is fascinating as well.

We don't know exactly when it started; we don't know why its form changed over time; we certainly don't know exactly when these words came to be wedded to this motion. When you look at who prays the sign of the cross today, you see amazing variety. South and Central American Catholics do it differently from North Americans. Orthodox Christians do it differently still and use a variety of phrasing, depending on the church.

The physical sign came first. From early in church history and for hundreds of years, Christians signed themselves and the world around them with crosses. This was an exceedingly odd thing to do, because in the Roman Empire, the cross represented a very shameful means of execution. One who died on a cross had obviously committed shameful acts and was enduring a justifiably shameful death, stripped naked, nailed and tied to wood, suffering to the scorn and mockery of passersby. Making the cross a central symbol of our faith at that time could be compared to making the electric chair a symbol of our faith today.

But with Jesus and those who share the Good News about him, this is the way things almost always are. As is his habit, God had done something new, had turned the world upside down, and had transformed shame into glory. In the cross, Christians saw it all: the power of sin, the tragedy of creation turned on its author, and in response, love sacrificial enough to embrace the tragedy and powerful enough to transform them.

So from the beginning, Christians spoke of the cross because Jesus had spoken of it, Jesus had hung on it, and Jesus had conquered it. The cross, weighted by the world's shame, was reverenced by Christians.

They not only spoke of the cross, they re-created it by making it their primary means of identification. It seems that the most common way to do this at first was with one finger, or perhaps the thumb, on the forehead. In the early third century, a North African Christian named Tertullian wrote:

> At every step and movement, whenever we come in or go out, in dressing or in putting on our shoes, at the bath, at table, at the lighting of the lamps, in going to rest, in sitting down, whatever employment occupies us we mark our foreheads with the sign of the cross.[1]

A century later, St. Cyril of Jerusalem indicated that the practice had expanded, so that the early Christians surrounded themselves and the air they breathed with crosses.

Let the cross become our seal, made with boldness by our fingers upon the forehead, oil everything on the bread we eat and the cups we drink; in our comings in and goings out; before sleep, when we lie down and when we awake; when we are walking and when we are still.[2]

At some point, Christians began making the sign of the cross in a more expansive way, over the entire body. We are not sure exactly when this development happened, because religious practice evolves over time, and tracing the evolution is difficult, especially when sources are scarce. Not only that, but none of this was happening by orders from the top; ordinary people were discovering powerful expressions of faith for themselves.

And, perhaps because the practice evolved rather than was officially introduced, it was done differently in different parts of the Christian world. Some believers moved their hands from the head to the heart, bringing to mind God's love. Others said that the hand should move from the head all the way down to the belly, to symbolize God's Word incarnate in the womb of Mary.

And what about the shoulders? For centuries, the movement throughout all of Christianity was from right to left, the way it is still done in Orthodox churches today. But during the Middle Ages some in the West started moving from left to right. Writing around the beginning of the thirteenth century, Pope Innocent III discussed both methods. He said that going from left to right was good because it symbolized Christ's descent from heaven (head) to earth (breast) and his crossing over from Jews (the right) to gentiles (the left). But on the other hand, going from left to right brought to mind the truth that Christ passed from death (the left—always the side with the most negative connections) to life (the right.)

Innocent III declared that both sequences were appropriate ways to make the sign of the cross. Eventually, though, in most of the West, the left-to-right system won out, although Spanish and Portuguese Catholics still go from right to left.

Hands, believe it or not, are another issue.

In most of the Western Church, we use an open hand to make the sign of the cross. Some scholars believe this happened as the faithful in congregations began to imitate the hand position of the priests who were blessing them. However, if you come from or are familiar with cultures rooted in Spain or with Orthodox practices, you know that this open hand isn't by any means universal. The positions of one's fingers are often weighted with an amazing amount of symbolism.

From the fifth through the eighth century, a heresy raged, especially in the Eastern parts of the church. The Monophysites taught that Jesus' human nature was absorbed into his divinity so he really had only one nature. It was especially popular in Egypt, where it began and where you can still find groups— Coptic and Ethiopian Christians, for example—that ascribe to it.

However, most Christians found this to be an incomplete understanding of Jesus. After all, if Jesus didn't have a real human nature, what meaning did his suffering on the cross have? And could he have really suffered at all?

Around this time, those Christians who believed that Jesus did indeed have both a human and divine nature started making the sign of the cross in a way that showed it: They signed with the index and third fingers joined together, symbolizing the dual nature of Christ.

Over the centuries, variations evolved. Some joined three fingers as a way of symbolizing the Trinity, or, with the same end in mind, they curved the last two fingers of their right hand over and then met them with their thumb. The two fingers that were left were extended, and those fingers, once again, symbolized Jesus' dual nature.

In the Russian Orthodox Church, the Christogram is used (it's also used by the pope when he extends a blessing). The fingers are arranged in a way to represent the contraction of "Jesus Christ" in Greek: IC XC. The index finger is extended to represent the *I,* the middle and last fingers are curved downward as the *C,* and the thumb crosses the second to the last finger to form the *X*.

In Spain and some Latin American countries, the sign of the cross has two parts: first a signing of the cross on the forehead, lips, and breast, then the large cross on head, breast and shoulders, followed by a kiss of the thumb, which has been crossed over the forefinger during the entire gesture, making, of course, one more cross.

And we haven't even gotten to the words yet!

It seems as if in those early days—back in the days of that simple cross on the forehead—Christians didn't associate any particular words with the making of the cross. Over time, they began to say things like "In the Name of Jesus" or "In the Name of the Holy Trinity." In the Russian Orthodox Church, it's accompanied by the Jesus Prayer:

"Lord" (head)

"Jesus Christ" (belly)

"Son of God" (right shoulder)

"Have Mercy on me a sinner." (left shoulder)

The Greek Orthodox often say, "Holy God, Holy Strong One, Holy Immortal One, Have Mercy on us."

And what about the Western Church? Here we invoke the Trinity as we make the sign of the cross. It is impossible to say for certain when this practice began, but it was common by at least the sixteenth century, when a Spanish priest named Navarro wrote:

> To bless ourselves is to make the sign of the cross over our-
> selves with three fingers passing from the forehead to the
> breast and from one side to the other. Sometimes we make
> no express invocation of the Blessed Trinity, as when we say
> *Deus in adjutorium,* or at the end of the *Gloria in excelsis,* or at
> the *Benedictio sit super nos* of the prayer in compline, and on
> many other occasions. At other times, however, we formally
> call upon the Blessed Trinity by these words: "In the name
> of the Father and of the Son and of the Holy Ghost."[3]

What's interesting is that even at this late date Navarro goes on to discuss the question of left to right or right to left, concluding that either is fine, making it clear that there was diversity in practice even then, as there is today.

Even a quick survey of the history of the sign of the cross might, and perhaps should, confound our assumptions of where so many of our Catholic practices come from. We sometimes imagine that everything about our tradition was at some point chiseled into stone by learned and determined authorities who then imposed them on the rest of us.

Not so. It was more like this: an impulse coursed through people in love with Christ. We are people bound to Jesus, whom God glorified through the cross. We want to identify ourselves, call down God's blessing, grace, and presence on ourselves and on our world, to claim it for him. We want to begin our days and our prayers "In the name . . ."

And we want to do this not just with words but with our bodies as well. In this prayer, which is the only Catholic prayer with a specific gesture attached to it, we express the truth that we are not mere spirit: we are body and soul, and God is the creator and redeemer of both.

In his novel *Brideshead Revisited,* Evelyn Waugh tells the story of an aristocratic British family whose members practice varying degrees of Catholic faith. At the end of the novel, the head of the family, Lord Marchmain, returns to England from Italy where he has lived for years with his mistress, outside the family, outside the home, outside his faith. He lies on his deathbed, incapacitated, unable to speak. Some in the family want to bring in the priest; others say no, it would be unwise and why bother anyway? Lord Marchmain is, in the words of the narrator, "a scoffer."

Finally, worn down by a determined daughter and the humble demeanor of the priest, the family let him in. The priest performs last rites and receives no response from Lord Marchmain. The priest tells Lord Marchmain that he will give him absolution and that he hopes that while he is doing so Lord Marchmain will be thinking about his sins.

> Suddenly, Lord Marchmain moved his hand to his forehead; I thought he had felt the touch of the chrism and was wiping it away. "O God," I prayed, "don't let him do that." But there was no need for fear; the hand moved slowly down his breast, then to his shoulder, and Lord Marchmain made the sign of the cross. Then I knew that the sign I had asked for was not a little thing, not a passing nod of recognition, and a phrase came back to me from my childhood of the veil of the temple being rent from top to bottom.[4]

The sign of the cross takes seconds to do, but in the knitting of words and action, spirit and flesh, lies power: power to communicate, power to bind us to God and to each other, power to bless, and power to signify, in the deepest way, the truth of redemption, and to bring it right down to where we are, here and now.

And so, in different places and times, reflecting new insights and growing concerns, this sign took shape, its every movement invested with rich meaning. And over time, not because anyone ordered it or legislated it but just because faithful people wanted to give expression to what they knew was true, this sign of the cross became our sign.

Romano Guardini was a spiritual writer of the early and mid-twentieth century who wrote deeply and profoundly about the Mass, the life of Jesus, and prayer. In his book, *Sacred Signs,* he said of the sign of the cross:

Think of these things when you make the sign of the cross. It is the holiest of all signs. Make a large cross, taking time, thinking what you do. Let it take in your whole being—body, soul, mind, will, thoughts, feelings, your doing and not-doing—and by signing it with the cross strengthen and consecrate the whole in the strength of Christ, in the name of the triune God.[5]

the our father

Our Father, who art in heaven,
    hallowed be thy name;
    thy kingdom come;
    thy will be done on earth as it is in heaven.
    Give us this day our daily bread;
    and forgive us our trespasses
    as we forgive those who trespass against us;
    and lead us not into temptation,
    but deliver us from evil.

Teach Us to Pray

There's no mystery concerning the origins of this prayer. Even the most skeptical Scripture scholars who make careers of expounding on what they think Jesus *didn't* say don't seem to have much of an argument here. They'll admit that if Jesus said anything, he said, "Our Father . . ."

He said it during those years in which he made his way around Palestine, stripping down faith to its core. He took those with ears to hear in and through the externals, exposing the depth of meaning at the heart of it all, taking us to the place where claiming less is knowing more.

Jesus broke open centuries of wondering at God's actions toward Israel and showed what great love was at the heart of those actions, showed how all of it had been building to the utter simplicity of God's kingdom. He took scads of laws—which rightfully shaped people into holiness—and revealed the single law at the center that leads to eternal life. He took all our worries about how to live and showed us birds in the field and a stranger bending over a man lying injured on a road. Live like this, he said.

He tore open prayer for us, too.

How should we pray, anyway? Once we decide that we belong to God and let ourselves be impressed with that sign of the cross, what next? How do we relate? How do we talk? How do we listen?

The apostles asked just this question, as Luke tells us in chapter 11 of his Gospel. We ask, along with the disciples, that Jesus teach us to pray. The answer is almost too simple, for the answer Jesus gives is a prayer.

> *Father, hallowed be your name,*
>> *your kingdom come.*
>> *Give us each day our daily bread*
>> *and forgive us our sins*
>> *for we ourselves forgive everyone in debt to us,*
>> *and do not subject us to the final test.*
>> (Luke 11:2–4)

Jesus follows this with just a bit of advice, not on technique or style or position, the things *we* tend to emphasize, but on attitude. It's as if he knows that we're not going to get it, that this is just too simple. So he tells a parable about a persistent friend and plays with an allegory about a father, a son, and a fish. A father wouldn't give a son a snake if he asked for a fish. Would God?

The prayer is found also in Matthew, in a slightly different context. It's in the Sermon on the Mount, after the Beatitudes and Jesus' explanation of the law. So far, Jesus has told his listeners to focus on the inner life: to remember that sin begins in the heart long before a person succumbs to action. When he talks about prayer, he keeps us focused inward—to pray in private, to avoid multiplying our words—and to say this:

Our Father in heaven,
  hallowed be your name,
  your kingdom come,
  your will be done,
    on earth as in heaven.
  Give us today our daily bread;
    and forgive us our debts,
    as we forgive our debtors;
    and do not subject us to the final test,
    but deliver us from the evil one.
  (Matthew 6:9–13)

Why two different versions? It's impossible to say for certain, but it's not hard to imagine that Jesus was often asked about prayer. Things probably haven't changed much in that regard. People want to be connected to God, and wonder how. So it's likely that as people questioned Jesus about prayer, he answered them by offering the same basic prayer, with a variation or two. You notice, for example, that the addition in Matthew, "your will be done, on earth as in heaven" is really just an explanation of what the previous phrase means. The coming of God's kingdom means that God's will be done.

In some Bibles—especially older translations, both Protestant and Catholic—you'll find yet another phrase at the end of Matthew's version.

For thine is the kingdom, and the power, and the glory, for ever.

The phrase is what's called a doxology, or words of praise that were commonly added to the ends of Jewish prayers. (Our Glory Be is an example of a Christian doxology.) The phrase is in a few Greek manuscripts, but not in any of those that scholars see as the "best"–those that are most reliably close to the original. It was probably a part of the ritual recitation by early Christians that crept into some versions of Matthew's Gospel. When Protestants pray the Lord's Prayer, they end it with "For the Kingdom . . ." and that phrase is part of a dialogue with the priest that Catholics say after we pray the Lord's Prayer at Mass.

This prayer that Jesus gives to us is, in terms of structure and content, very similar to traditional Jewish prayer. There is actually nothing in it that a good Jew of Jesus' time couldn't pray, which should not surprise us, given that he was a Jewish man talking about prayer to other Jews.

The prayer begins by honoring God and is, in essence, a prayer for God's rule to come to earth, a theme of prayers such as the Eighteen Benedictions, prayers of blessing that a good Jew was to say three times a day and which some historians have suggested was replaced by Jesus' Our Father in the lives of his Jewish disciples.[1]

The prayer strays just a bit from tradition, though, focusing us in a way that Jesus did throughout his preaching, revealing the newness of the Good News and calling us to address God as Father.

Jewish prayers did begin with God's name–not the name revealed to Abraham that was to remain unspoken, of course, but other titles—and often quite a few of them strung together. Jesus, by beginning his prayer with only a single title, tells us that only one is necessary: *abba,* which is startling because that word is never used to address God in Jewish prayer. Tradition sometimes referred to God as a father but never *addressed* God as "father," much less with this informal title, which really means "papa."[2]

It's the gospel in two words, really: *Our Father.* God gives us life and sustains us in love and mercy, and this love binds us to God as children to a father and to one another as brothers and sisters. Eternally. Period.

So right here, we see what Jesus is up to. Yes, he wants us to say these words when we pray, certainly, but just as important he wants us to take this attitude and to imbue all our prayer with it, no matter what specific words are attached.

How do we pray? Well, simply recall who God is and who we are to him, and pray. Talk. Be a child to a father. Be persistent, as Jesus says in Luke (11:5–8). Keep it simple, as he says in Matthew (6:7–8).

But what do we pray for? That's another sticky question.

Your kingdom come, your will be done.

Why do we pray, anyway? Are our prayers about understanding God's will and letting it guide us? Or are we really, at heart, trying to bring God around to our way of thinking and convince him to approve our decisions?

The disciples asked Jesus how to pray. He answered them simply, giving them a model: Trust in God as your loving parent, pray that his will be done in your lives and in the world, and then ask him to provide for your needs, forgive your sins, and protect you when you are tempted and tested.

What more do we need?

From the beginning, Christians took to heart Jesus' gift of this prayer. The version that appears in Matthew, along with that doxology, appears in one of the earliest instructions for Christians, a document called the *Didache,* which scholars date somewhere between the late first and mid-second centuries. Along with a lot of other advice and teaching about the celebration of the Lord's Supper and the moral stance of the Christian, the document, which probably emerged from Christian communities in Syria, quotes Matthew's version of the Our Father and instructs the reader to "pray in this way three times a day."

The prayer of Jesus was taught to catechumens—people preparing for baptism and the Christian life—but only very close to the time of their baptism (at that time, baptism happened during the Easter Vigil) and recited by them for the first time during their first participation in the entire celebration of the Eucharist. Remember that during this time in the early church not just anyone could attend the eucharistic liturgy, much less the whole liturgy from beginning to end. The unbaptized could be in attendance up through the Scriptures and the homily, but then they had to leave. The Eucharist, or "the mysteries," was reserved only for the baptized, as was the recitation of this prayer of Jesus.

Jesus' prayer had a place in eucharistic celebrations from early on, a place that was confirmed and specified in the Roman liturgies of the late sixth century by Pope Gregory the Great. He directed that this prayer should be recited right after the canon, or eucharistic prayer, and before what we call the "fraction," which is the moment in the Mass in which the presider breaks the Host and we sing the *Agnus Dei*, or Lamb of God. This is exactly where the prayer is said in the eucharistic celebration today, fourteen centuries later.

Gregory gave voice to additional reasons to include Jesus' prayer at this point in the liturgy. He said it was most appropriate to pray the prayer Jesus taught in the very real presence of his body and blood. Later theologians went deeper, as theologians like to do. The prayer is about submission to the Father's will, which is exactly what Jesus' sacrifice on the cross was all about. They also appreciated the connection between "daily bread" and the Bread of Life that nourishes us spiritually.[3]

Christians throughout history haven't prayed the Our Father only at Mass; it's been a vital, fundamental part of individual personal prayer as well. And one of the most interesting points about it is that for centuries, most Christians—even the uneducated and illiterate—prayed it in Latin, long after Latin had died as the language of common conversation.

In Latin, the Our Father is translated *Pater Noster*. Up until the Protestant Reformation, Western European Christians hardly ever prayed their memorized prayers in any other language but Latin, either in or out of Mass, and the Pater Noster and the Ave Maria were the prayers they recited most frequently, along with the Credo (the Creed). Christians were expected to know these prayers by heart. Vernacular versions were widely available and were used in preaching and teaching, but when it came to saying the words, Latin was still the language of the church, government, and education. We can see from late medieval primers that even schoolchildren were taught these three prayers in Latin as soon as they had learned the alphabet.

Numerous church councils and bishops' instructions made clear the duty of preachers and teachers to help the people understand what these Latin words meant. It was, in fact, a convenient and concise way to teach the faith. If people could understand these prayers, they reasoned, particularly the Pater and the Credo, they were getting an education in the basics of the Christian faith.

For those committed to deepening their spiritual lives, to growing in intimacy with God through meditation and contemplation, the Our Father was one of the many prayers suggested as a means to this end. The goal of our prayer life is always to draw near to God in a pure presence that is beyond words. Most of us can't just enter into that state of intimacy without guidance and preparation, and we always have been able to depend on vocal prayer and the Scriptures.

So while the Our Father was a foundation to help Christians understand their faith, it was also one of those vital means to deeper relationship with God. Praying the words of the Our Father in a meditative way was often suggested as an invaluable step on this journey.

St. Teresa of Ávila is one of the great spiritual teachers of the Christian tradition. Living in Spain in the sixteenth century, she led a reform of religious life and wrote books on prayer and spirituality that have lost nothing of their truth and power over the centuries. In *The Way of Perfection,* she encouraged her sisters to depend on the Our Father in their prayer:

> So well composed by the good Master was it, daughters, that each of us may use it in her own way. I am astounded when I consider that in its few words are enshrined all contemplation and perfection, so that if we study it no other book seems necessary. For thus far in the Paternoster the Lord has taught us the whole method of prayer and of high contemplation, from the very beginnings of mental prayer, to Quiet and Union. . . . It has occurred to me that, as this prayer was meant to be a general one for the use of all, so that everyone could interpret it as he thought right, ask for what he wanted and find comfort in doing so.[4]

The Pater Noster came into play in personal devotion in Christian history in another way as well: through what we now call the rosary. While we think of the rosary as being a prayer centered on Mary, in its origins, it wasn't.

Christians from a Jewish background brought with them the tradition of using the Psalms in prayer, which eventually settled into the practice of trying to pray all 150 Psalms over the course of a week, especially in monastic settings.

People outside of monasteries, and even some of the monks who engaged in more manual labor than others, didn't have the time or perhaps the learning to join in these ancient prayers, so the practice evolved of saying 150 Pater Nosters instead, then subsequently, of fashioning loops of knotted strings or beads to keep track of them. Eventually, as we'll see in the chapter on the Hail Mary, these prayers and the manner of saying them evolved into what we now know as the rosary. There's a road in London that's still called Paternoster Row, because it was the center of the rosary-making industry in the city.

And that word, *patter*? It's derived from this very prayer, evoked by the rapid recitation of the word *pater* over and over again.

So what happened? When did people start saying "Our Father" instead of "Pater Noster," especially in their private prayers?

For English speakers, it happened as a result of the Reformation. In 1534 King Henry VIII broke from the Roman Catholic Church and declared himself head of the Church of England. Just a couple of years later, he decreed that the people should be taught the Lord's Prayer in English, and eventually was forced, because of the confusion of a multiplicity of translations, to issue a standard, approved translation, in the *Royal Primer* of 1545.

In 1553, Henry's still Roman Catholic daughter Mary became queen. During her short time on the throne she tried to reinstate Catholic practices (and persecuted dissenters in the process, just as her father had persecuted Roman Catholics), but there was never any effort to get people to start saying the Our Father in Latin again. So, ironically, the translation that Catholics used then and now is that promulgated by the king who broke away from the Roman Catholic Church.[5]

Just as oddly, even as we have modernized so much of the language we use in prayer—the "Holy Ghost" has become the "Holy Spirit," and many have dropped the archaic "thee" and "thy" from the Hail Mary—we've not adjusted the Our Father one bit. We still say "art in heaven" and "hallowed be thy name," and most of us, even if we harbor no nostalgia for the liturgies of old, would probably be at a loss if the order came down to start saying, "who is in heaven." I know I would.

One night when I was thirteen, a mysterious, terrifying something awakened me from the depths of adolescent sleep. You know how it is when that happens: You are thrust into a foggy haze and have no idea what is going on but are acutely afraid.

Immediately, I started praying the Our Father. It shot out of my lips, *thy*s and *art*s intact, as my mother had taught me, as her mother had taught her, and so on. The words came tumbling out before I could even begin to take hold of rational thought. But once things settled down, even rational thought was of limited value because, truth be told, earthquakes are not a common feature of life in Knoxville, Tennessee, but that's exactly what I was experiencing.

I grabbed onto the Lord's Prayer that night for the same reason that so many of us return to it over and over again, this, the first prayer that we're taught. It's a capsule expression of everything we need to know and live by, given to us by Jesus himself. It captures our relationship to God: what we want it to be, what we hope it can be, what it is. Through it, Jesus teaches us how to pray, and since Paul has told us we're to "pray without ceasing" (1 Thessalonians 5:17), that means that through this prayer Jesus also teaches us how to live.

hail
mary

Hail Mary, full of grace. The Lord is with thee. Blessed art thou amongst women, and blessed is the fruit of thy womb, Jesus. Holy Mary, Mother of God, pray for us sinners, now and at the hour of our death. Amen.

Greeting Our Mother

I would never claim to be an expert in All Things Catholic All the Time, but I have seen a lot and read a great deal, and I like to think that nothing much would surprise me.

But pinning money on Mary—that surprised me a little.

It was the Feast of the Assumption, known in Cleveland's Little Italy neighborhood simply as "The Feast," an occasion to celebrate not only Mary but Italian culture as well. We were there on a little summer excursion.

Mass was followed by a procession, at the center of which was a large but ordinary statue of Mary. She was attended by a young woman who had been up there on the platform, in her Sunday best, unsmiling, for at least an hour before the procession began, taking dollar bills in various denominations that were thrust at her by the crowd and pinning them to every empty space available on the platform—ribbons, bouquets, everything. As the cart was hauled down the street, amid banners and children dressed up like saints and Italian peasants, Mary floated, it seemed, in clouds of money.

To an outsider, the scene might represent the worst expressions of Catholic devotion to Mary: borderline idolatry tinged with superstition, and just a little opportunism.

But maybe there's more to it than that. Mary—friend, mother, sister—is worth our time, worthy of some recognition, deserving of some gratitude. Catholic devotion to Mary certainly may be all over the map and, at times, take on a distorted role, but its origins and basic impulse are sound and solidly rooted. Mary was chosen by God to be the mother of Jesus. Reserving a place for Mary in our faith life isn't an end in itself. She reminds us constantly that redemption is not just about ideas or abstractions. She was the physical mother of the Savior, and also his first disciple. She shows us who Jesus is—fully human, as well as divine. And she reveals who we will be—human beings but partakers in the very life of God.

The most important Mary-centered prayer expresses the basic simplicity and gospel focus of devotion to Mary. Confronted with our own questions about Marian devotion, not to speak of outsiders' wondering about Mary and her dollars, it's useful and necessary to return often to the Hail Mary.

Our story begins in the first chapter of Luke's Gospel. An angel, Gabriel by name, appears to this Jewish girl and says, "Hail, favored one! The Lord is with you" (Luke 1:28).

If you look at various translations of this verse, you'll find some differences in how that first part is worded. Some will say "Peace be with you" or "Rejoice" and will render Mary's identification as "favored woman."

When the early Christians, who were increasingly using Latin as their common language, were translating the books of Scripture, they considered how Greek, the original language of the Gospels, might best be communicated in their own language. The general sense of that first verse from Luke is that the angel is greeting Mary and telling her that she is highly blessed and favored by God. The early church fathers described God's favor in terms of "grace," and so they translated accordingly:

Ave, gratia plena!

Which literally means, "Hail, full of grace!" These words became the common way to repeat this passage and eventually worked their way into prayer.

The second part is also a greeting, but not from an angel. Mary's cousin Elizabeth, miraculously pregnant with her own baby, greets Mary as she comes for a visit: "Most blessed are you among women, and blessed is the fruit of your womb" (Luke 1:42).

So it really makes sense that, in the evolving prayer life of the church, people would make a connection between these two greetings offered to Mary, and join them as they were moved to greet Mary themselves.

This didn't happen for a very long time. We have evidence of the greeting being a part of one prayer (on the Fourth Sunday of Advent) in the liturgy of Rome, and it's found inscribed on an Egyptian pottery shard from the sixth century. Prayers directed to Mary did exist during this period. Looking at various liturgies from the Eastern and Western Churches, the works of theologians, we find many words of supplication to Mary, and even as early as the late third century, a Christian church was dedicated to her in Alexandria, Egypt.[1]

But as far as this greeting goes, we've really no evidence of it being used in individual prayer until around the eleventh century, when something called the Little Office of the Blessed Virgin Mary appeared.

Men and women who live in religious communities have from earliest days in the church committed themselves to regular ritual prayer throughout the day and even into the night. It's called the Divine Office or the Liturgy of the Hours. By the sixth century, the most common structure was that of eight prayer times, from Matins in the middle of the night, to Compline, before bed. The center of these prayers, recited together or individually, was the Psalms.

In the eleventh century, some monks started adding to the office a set of prayers centering on Mary, perhaps first out of personal preference. It didn't take long for these prayers to grow in popularity and even beyond the monastery walls. By the beginning of the twelfth century, we have plenty of evidence— from devotional manuscripts and even legends of men or women who received help from Mary because they recited her "Little Office"–that this relatively short devotion was a part of life for many Christians, whether religious or laity. It was one way that those in the world could join in the constant prayer of the monks.

This Little Office was composed of psalms that had a particular echo of themes in Mary's life and in her role as the Mother of the Savior, as well as the frequent repetition of that angelic greeting: *Ave Maria, gratia plena, Dominus tecum, Benedicta tu in mulieribus,* recited either as a whole phrase or antiphonally, sometimes paired with Elizabeth's greeting. Somewhere along the line, "Maria" was added to the angel's greeting, an addition which, if you say it aloud, not only makes the identification clearer but improves the poetic rhythm as well.[2]

It didn't take long, then, for the Ave Maria to get separated from the rest of the Little Office and take hold as a popular prayer all by itself. This happened at the same time that devotion to the Virgin was growing by leaps and bounds.

She'd always been honored, a stance that was crystallized in the fifth century, when church councils, digging deep and hard to try to resolve and understand how Jesus could be fully divine and fully human, confirmed that Jesus was, indeed one person with these two natures, combined in some mysterious, yet necessary way.

And what did this have to do with Mary? If Jesus was who he was—fully divine and fully human—then this meant that Mary could indeed be called *Theotokos,* as she was frequently being referred to in the Eastern Church: "mother of God."

From this point it began, the growth of Christianity's attention to Mary's role in salvation history. As the Middle Ages blossomed, so did this devotion. Christians valued Mary because she was one of them; her life held the promise and potential that any one of theirs could, but because she was the mother of God, she was in an especially worthy place. God the Father, often presented in the person of a frightening king or judge, was too daunting to approach. So Christians turned to Mary.

And so art, music, and prayer with Mary at the center blossomed. It's in this context that the Ave Maria dislodged itself and floated free of the Little Office, finding its way onto the lips of countless petitioners seeking help and comfort, often praying fifty or a hundred *Aves* at a time, particularly in the monasteries, accompanied by genuflection or even prostration. St. Margaret of Hungary (d. 1271), besides threatening to cut off her lips and nose upon learning that the pope was cooperating with her father the king in trying to force a marriage on her, was reputed to have said, at times, a thousand Aves a day, prostrating each time.

But what of the second half of the prayer?

As the popularity of the Ave Maria grew, along with it grew a sense that this was not actually a prayer; it was a greeting. So, quite often, a prayer or intention was added to the end of it— some kind of appeal for Mary's help or prayers. We find scattered evidence of this practice throughout the early Middle Ages, and firm examples by the mid- to late fifteenth century.

Scholars believe that it all came together, strange to say, in the works of a man who, in Florence in 1498, was hung and burned as a heretic and uncomfortably vocal political critic. His name was Girolamo Savonarola. He was Dominican, a self-proclaimed prophet and an intense critic of church and political leaders (which explains the hanging and burning). It's in his writings—some of which were quite brilliant and thoroughly orthodox—that we find the complete prayer (except for one word: *nostrae*) that wound up being the official Ave Maria approved by the church and placed in the church's prayer book, the Roman Breviary. Pope Pius V published the breviary in 1568 to standardize the prayer of the church in the chaos and uncertainty of the years after the Reformation.

The Ave Maria has made its way into other devotions over the years. The most well-known is the rosary, but as we noted in the previous chapter, long before Christians were repeating Aves in groups of fifty or a hundred, they were repeating Pater Nosters as a way of participating in the prayers of the 150 Psalms in the monasteries.

What happened? There's no straight line of development, as is so often the case with Catholic prayer. Different habits and practices evolved all over Europe, winding their way together and being teased apart in new ways over hundreds of years. Some started saying their Pater Nosters on beads to keep track and interspersing them with Aves in a pattern. During the fourteenth and fifteenth centuries, the image of roses and a rose garden came to be increasingly associated with Mary, and collections of prayers and devotions centered on the Virgin were referred to as garlands of prayers or *rosarium:* "rose garden."

Others used these sets of repeated prayers as a way to deepen our connection with the mysteries of Christ's life. Some suggested praying in front of a picture as an aid to meditation, or they attached specific meditations to each set of prayers, culminating in the early fifteenth century with a work by Dominic of Prussia, who attached the Ave Maria to meditation points on the life of Christ:

Hail Mary, full of grace, the Lord is with you, blessed are you among women, and blessed is the fruit of your womb, Jesus Christ whose feet Mary Magdalen washed with her tears, and wiped with her hair, kissed and anointed. Amen.[3]

The process culminated with official Church approval of the rosary. In 1571, the use of the rosary was credited in the defeat of Turkish forces at Lepanto, and a year later, Pope Pius V created The Feast of the Most Holy Rosary, to be celebrated on October 7. The next pope, Gregory XIII, issued a prayer book which included the rosary in the form we know it today—fifteen decades of Hail Marys interspersed with Our Fathers and other prayers, during which we're called to meditate on three sets of mysteries: joyful, sorrowful, and glorious, enriched in 2002 by Pope John Paul II's addition of the luminous mysteries, which are centered on Jesus' public ministry.

The Hail Mary is all over the place in Catholic life. Besides the rosary, it's a part of the Angelus, a sequence of prayers that was said for centuries by many Catholics at morning, noon, and night. At various times throughout history, the Hail Mary was incorporated into the Mass, most frequently at the time of the Prayers of the Faithful or as a part of prayers said after Mass.[4] And of all traditional Catholic prayers, the Hail Mary is probably the one most frequently set to music.

Catholicism is often characterized in the popular mind as a religion of hierarchy, rigidity, and strictly imposed order. People who are Catholic know better. The function of human authority in this church has more often than not been as arbiter concerning beliefs and practices that have bubbled up "from below," and the history of the Hail Mary, and Marian devotion in general, makes this clear.

Eleventh-century Catholics weren't ordered by a bishop to start recognizing Mary as a part of their spiritual lives. They wanted to, so they did. No commission declared that it would be most advisable to add some intercessions to this greeting, but people did that, spontaneously, over a couple of centuries in different areas of Europe.

Christians just knew—they knew that Mary said something important to them about Jesus and about their own present and future. The basic impulse behind this prayer isn't worship, as some, both outside and inside the church, mistakenly believe. It's recognition that we can turn to Mary, as we can to any faithful fellow disciple, and ask her to intercede with God on our behalf.

And while I still don't completely "get" the money on the statue, I do think I understand why the custom exists. After all, when someone helps you understand your life and faith, the least you can do is say thank you, with whatever you have on hand. Flowers, candles, words—even a little cash.

credo

The Apostles' Creed

I believe in God, the Father almighty,
  creator of heaven and earth.
I believe in Jesus Christ, his only Son, our Lord.
  He was conceived by the power of the Holy Spirit
    and born of the Virgin Mary.
  He suffered under Pontius Pilate,
    was crucified, died, and was buried.
  He descended to the dead.
  On the third day he rose again.
  He ascended into heaven,
    and is seated at the right hand of the Father.
  He will come again to judge the living and the dead.

I believe in the Holy Spirit,
>   the holy catholic Church,
>   the communion of saints,
>   the forgiveness of sins,
>   the resurrection of the body,
>   and the life everlasting. Amen.

The Nicene Creed

We believe in one God,
>   the Father, the Almighty,
>   maker of heaven and earth,
>   of all that is, seen and unseen.

We believe in one Lord, Jesus Christ,
>   the only Son of God,
>   eternally begotten of the Father,
>   God from God, Light from Light,
>   true God from true God,
>   begotten, not made, one in Being with the Father.
>   Through him all things were made.
>   For us men and for our salvation
>   he came down from heaven:

by the power of the Holy Spirit
>   he was born of the Virgin Mary, and became man.

For our sake he was crucified under Pontius Pilate;
>   he suffered, died, and was buried.
>   On the third day he rose again

in fulfillment of the Scriptures;
he ascended into heaven
and is seated at the right hand of the Father.
He will come again in glory to judge the living and the
dead,
and his kingdom will have no end.
We believe in the Holy Spirit, the Lord, the giver of life,
who proceeds from the Father and the Son.
With the Father and the Son he is worshiped and
glorified.
He has spoken through the Prophets.
We believe in one holy catholic and apostolic Church.
We acknowledge one baptism for the forgiveness of
sins.
We look for the resurrection of the dead,
and the life of the world to come. Amen.

What We Believe

I spend a great deal of my time trying to communicate with three people ages twelve, eighteen, and twenty-one. They all have their charms, but one really irritating thing about talking with them is that it takes twice as long as it should to get a straight answer from any of them. I don't think they lie, but they exhibit a consistent and thorough commitment to sarcasm.

A typical phone conversation with my middle son, a freshman in college, is composed of variations on this kind of exchange: "You are going to class, aren't you?" "No, Mom, I'm skipping every day. Haven't been to class in a week."

There are times, with him and with the others, that I literally have to threaten to hang up or walk out of the room in order to get them to cut it out, which they then do, cheerfully chastened. I'm all for hilarity, but more than that, I'm for reality, and that's what I want all my relationships to be based on: real people being realistic about their real lives.

Loving God isn't—or shouldn't be—any different. That might be hard to tell from the current zeitgeist. These days the spiritual life is not so much about attaching yourself to something absolutely, astonishingly real and allowing yourself to be shaped by that real thing, but more about simply labeling as divine anything that makes you feel better about life.

Not so, according to the vast weight of Christian tradition, and to most other religious traditions as well. God is—I am Who

Am as revealed to Abraham. God is not defined by my wishes or wants. God *is*.

Enter creeds, those concise (relatively speaking), authorized professions of faith that help us keep reality at the center of our faith relationship with God. The word *creed* comes from the Latin word *credo,* which means "I believe." Creeds are the fruit of intense, sometimes contentious reflection on the question of who this God really is and what he has really said—words real enough to stake our lives on.

For Roman Catholicism and many other Christian bodies, the most important creeds are the Apostles' and the Nicene. The use of either is permitted at Sunday Roman Catholic Mass, although it's usually the Nicene that we end up saying. We normally say the Apostles' Creed when we pray the rosary, as well.

The Apostles' Creed is earlier in origins, but probably not by much, and despite some pious legends to the contrary, it wasn't actually written by the apostles.

The content of faith was important to Christians from the earliest days. They weren't preaching platitudes or hypotheticals. They were preaching about their friend and teacher Jesus, who lived and saved. The invitation to join the way wasn't a call to hook up with a great group of people. It was a call to embrace the truth—one truth that was out there, because God is One: "As you were also called to the one hope of your call; one Lord, one faith, one baptism, one God and Father of all, who is over all and through all and in all" (Ephesians 4:4–6).

So naturally, professing your belief in this "one faith" was a crucial part of the "one baptism." The evidence indicates that from the beginning, a profession of faith was part of the baptismal ritual, either as questions asked—sort of like what we do today when we renew our baptismal vows—or as a set of statements recited right before baptism.

All of these baptismal professions had a threefold structure, in imitation of Jesus' words on baptism in Matthew 28. "Go, therefore, and make disciples of all nations, baptizing them in the name of the Father, and of the Son, and of the holy Spirit" (Matthew 28:19). That was the core of this Christian faith: belief in the triune God and all that it implies. All Christian creeds are elaborations of this basic structure, and that tells you what's essential about the Christian faith.

As a process for the formation of new Christians developed, so did these formulas. By the fifth century, we see that in some parts of the church there was a special day of "scrutiny" on which the profession of faith was imparted to the catechumens, and the presiding bishop instructed them on its meaning. After memorizing the profession of faith, then, the catechumen would recite it right before he or she was baptized.[1]

What we now say as the Apostles' Creed took its final shape around 700, but we find professions of faith very close to it by the third century, in almost identical forms in both Gaul (what is today France and parts of Belgium) and North Africa.

Our impulse to define the basis of a relationship with another person hardly ever comes out of the blue. It's usually prompted by something: an occasion, an event, or a challenge. Our creeds evolve in somewhat the same way. They come to birth because what they say needs to be said. New believers need clear statements of what they're entering into. And errors need to be corrected.

Our Christian creeds (and there are several) have usually taken shape in the context of conflict. A thinker or preacher or movement emerges that says something about God that isn't true, that violates the ancient understanding of faith passed on by the apostles. Clarification of exactly why this is so, and of what it means to be Christian becomes more than a good idea; it's now a necessity for the sake of truth and unity.

During the time that the Apostles' Creed evolved, in the second through fourth centuries, one of the major challenges to Christianity, even from within, was gnosticism. Gnosticism was an intellectual and spiritual movement that, when stripped down to its basics, declared that the material world, created by a bad god, was evil, and the spirit world, created by a good god, was good.

Christians who incorporated gnostic threads into their faith were more than skeptical of Jesus' human nature. Some versions proposed that Jesus' body wasn't real, and all affirmed that his role in salvation was as the one who imparts secret knowledge (often in the form of arcane words and formulas) that we need to know to free our spirits from the imprisonment of material bodies.

This ideology was no idle threat, either. Beginning in the mid-second century, gnostic thinking was all over the place, including inside the Christian church. It's not only arcane and elitist, it also makes a mockery of the Incarnation. At the worst it makes Jesus out to be a liar, at the best. a good actor—but not a person whose life, death, and bodily resurrection could be the means of our salvation.

So the Apostles' Creed was formed in the years when gnostic heresies threatened the unity of the church. The creed responds to this threat by emphasizing God's relationship to the earth and the reality of Jesus' bodily existence. It tells us that what Jesus gives is not secret knowledge but forgiveness of sins for all. It tells us that our bodies aren't fake or evil; they're real, and in Christ, they are sanctified for eternal life.

Gnosticism hasn't gone away; we in the West just don't name it as such anymore. We're acting like Gnostics when we live as though we can do anything we desire with our bodies without our souls being affected. We employ a gnostic attitude when we turn to groups that revolve around esoteric and elitist sensibilities. When we seek Jesus as an idea, rather than as person whose life was like ours in all ways but sin, we're toying with Gnosticism, and praying the Apostles' Creed can be just the tonic we need.

Jesus' dual nature is of course a mystery. A knotty, sometimes aggravating mystery, and one that Christianity had to work hard to articulate in ways that were understandable and absolutely faithful to what the Gospels tell us. These creeds of the early church are the fruits of that struggle. The Apostles' Creed reflects the church's response to the temptation to tip the balance against Jesus' humanity. When Jesus' divinity came under fire, the Nicene Creed evolved.

Arius was a priest from Alexandria, Egypt, who, early in the fourth century, started preaching and teaching that Jesus wasn't fully divine, that he was, in fact, a created being. He may have been at a higher level, a "son of God" in a way that the rest of us are not, but still created by God, not fully sharing in God's nature.

Arianism was popular. It was a seemingly easy way in and out of the mystery of Jesus, and more than a few bishops embraced it. The fierce battle over Arianism ended up lasting almost two hundred years, as church councils, emperors, bishops, and ordinary people entered the fray, sometimes violently.

The first church council to deal with Arianism was the Council of Nicaea, convened in 325 by the Emperor Constantine I (who was himself only a catechumen at the time) in Nicaea, a town that's in present-day Turkey. The bishops who met there discussed Arianism and determined that it was not consistent with the picture of Jesus in the Gospels, and so they emerged with a statement of authentic faith that's basically the first part of the Nicene Creed. You can see the concern of these bishops emerging through the phrases and the words: *God from God, Light from Light, true God from true God, begotten, not made, one in Being with the Father.*

The purpose of that phrase is to remind us that the truth the Gospels attest to, while hard to understand, is about God becoming flesh. It may strike us as excessively philosophical language, but remember that the nature of the challenge itself–

Arianism—was philosophical, playing off of notions of "being" and "essence," so the response had to draw on the same kind of language.

And just as with the gnostic problem, you can see the importance of the discussion at Nicaea. If Jesus wasn't fully God, then . . . what? What importance would his crucifixion have but symbolic? What would Jesus be but a good man, a prophet, and teacher, which is all well and good, but we already have a lot of those.

The rest of the Nicene Creed was obviously modeled after other professions of faith. It took its final form around 451, when yet another council, the Council of Chalcedon, was convened to handle Arianism once and for all, and confirmed the truth of the creeds that had emerged from both the Council of Nicaea in 325 and the Council of Constantinople in 381.

We saw that the Apostles' Creed was rooted in, and was predominantly used as, a statement of faith in relation to baptism. The Nicene Creed was used as a baptismal profession in some places, too, but its most frequent use was in the same place we see it today: at Mass.

We see the Nicene Creed recited at Mass here and there during the sixth century in Constantinople (now Istanbul, then the center of Christianity in the East), and even in Spain. Around 800, Charlemagne, the ruler who'd been given the title of "Emperor of the Holy Roman Empire" by a pope and whose kingdom was really the beginnings of that amalgamation of church and state we call Christendom, ordered that the Nicene Creed be inserted into the Mass as said in his kingdom.

He did this with the permission of Pope Leo III, but we can't help but notice the role that secular rulers felt free to play in church affairs; it was simply a fact of life during this time. They convened councils, deposed bishops, and even made rules for the celebration of the liturgy. This quite interesting and long-lived relationship between secular leaders and church affairs is rather useful to remember when people try to tell us that church structure as we know it in the twenty-first century is an immutable, untouchable thing. Not quite.

But the Nicene Creed didn't make its way into the Mass as celebrated in Rome (which was the defining center of liturgical life for most of the West) until the eleventh century. In fact, one of Charlemagne's successors, Henry II, traveled to Rome in 1014 and expressed surprise that there was no Credo prayed at Mass. The Roman clerics sniffed and retorted that because Rome had never been disturbed by heresy, there was no need to recite this creed.[2] But the pope, ultimately influenced by the emperor, ordered its placement, and there we have it, as a faith-filled response to the Liturgy of the Word and preparation for the Liturgy of the Eucharist. As scholar Luke Timothy Johnson puts it:

> The creed draws the readings of Scripture into a focus on the central mystery of the incarnation and redemption and

the hope of a blessed resurrection. Thus it draws the gathered faithful to a clear focus and a shared commitment before they enter the sacred mystery of the Lord's Supper.[3]

In relationships of all kinds there are times when we have to remind ourselves of who the other person really is and why we love him or her. At night, we go into a difficult child's room and watch him sleep, letting his calm, peaceful expression remind us of his essential goodness and potential. We try to forget, for just a few minutes, why we're so angry at a spouse or a friend and consciously remind ourselves of who that person really is.

This is what creeds do for us as individuals and as a church. When we pray a creed, we're in the presence of God, reminding ourselves of who God really is when we're tempted to build him up in our own image. In praying the creed we dispose ourselves to deepen our friendship with God because we're committed to loving him as he is, not as we would like him to be.

In other words, as we join in the ancient words of the creed, we're committing ourselves to a love that's based on the reality of the Beloved. Personally, I find anything less not really worth giving my Sunday mornings for, much less, my life.

the morning offering

O Jesus, through the Immaculate Heart of Mary, I offer you all my prayers, works, joys, and sufferings of this day in union with the holy sacrifice of the Mass throughout the world. I offer them for all the intentions of your Sacred Heart: the salvation of souls, reparation for sin, the reunion of all Christians. I offer them for the intentions of our bishops and of all apostles of prayer—in particular for those recommended by our Holy Father this month.

The Gift of the Present Moment

"Be careful, or you'll wish your life away."

I was nineteen, sitting in the office at the University's Catholic student parish, talking to the secretary. I was griping about being overwhelmed with reading and papers, all the tests I had looming, and saying how much I wished the semester was over, so I could just relax. I remember the secretary like a photograph, peering over half-moon glasses, reprimanding me in smoke-drenched Jersey tones.

"Be careful," she barked, "or you'll wish your life away."

A lot of professors tried to tell me a lot of things during those four years. I hardly remember any of them. But I remember that—almost every day, too.

Perhaps I remember because wishful thinking is my particular weakness. Everything will be okay once I get this book written, this kitchen cleaned, or this kid out of diapers. I'll certainly be happier when my oldest figures out his life and stops worrying me with it, or when we can move back south or when the weekend rolls around.

Or at least when it's ten o'clock and everyone's asleep and I can have some peace.

But here I am now, all kids officially out of diapers, a thousand weekends come and gone, the kitchen cleaned a million times, too many chaotic late afternoons and yearned-for peaceful evenings faded into dark night. Here I am, a quarter-century away from the girl in that office, still wishing, although I know

I shouldn't, still having to force myself to live in the present, because that's all I have. And if I spend it wishing that it were another place and time, I'll miss it.

Living in the present isn't just a nice sentiment, good for a best-selling self-help book or two. It's profoundly Christian and can be translated to this: God is with you here, now.

More than a century ago, some seminarians engaged in some wishful thinking, themselves. They didn't mind where they were, but they were exceedingly anxious to get somewhere else, and out of that experience came a prayer that grounds us, that gently turns us to the present and its possibilities. This prayer is very good to say in the morning, when the specter of another tense day at work or one more hectic round of errands, car pools, lessons, and fights, or even long hours of pain and loneliness, stretch ahead.

So calling this prayer the Morning Offering is appropriate, although its contemporary enthusiasts would like it to be called the Daily Offering. It sets us straight no matter what time of day we say it, and it roots us in reality, even the reality we may not see.

The story begins in 1844, at a Jesuit seminary in France. A lot of the seminarians were already scheduled to head for missionary work in India, and the prospect delighted them. They simply could not get enough of India. They talked about India, they wondered about India, and they scoured the library for information about India.

Their superiors were not exactly pleased, however, for in the throes of their enthusiasm, the seminarians were neglecting the tasks at hand: their studies, which at that point mostly concerned systematic theology and New Testament Greek and unfortunately had little direct relationship to India.

So, we're told, their superior got control of the situation and gave the seminarians a talk. Right now, he said, your mission is not in India. Right now, your mission is here, in your classrooms, in your studies. Some versions say that this Father Gautrelet made his appeal on the day of the Feast of St. Francis Xavier, the great Jesuit missionary to India and the Far East, and perhaps he did.[1]

What evolved out of this experience was the prayer we call the Morning Offering. The seminarians themselves put it together out of what they were being taught and what they hoped for, and you can see this, for it is tinged with a definite missionary sensibility. This is not a prayer that is looking inward for strength. It is a prayer that directs our gaze outward, for purpose.

Many more than Jesuit seminarians pray it now. It's been popularized and spread throughout the world by an organization called the Apostleship of Prayer that emerged in the same time and place as the Morning Offering. The Apostleship of Prayer is enormous, involving tens of millions of Catholics around the world who work to bring the Good News to the world through prayer. And it recommends the Morning Offering to its members.

The prayer's wording sets it apart from others we've considered in this book, and not, perhaps, in a good way. It didn't evolve organically; it's very clearly composed, and not by a passionate mystic. In other words, it's rather formal and has a bit of a laundry-list feel about it. It may not exactly grab my heart, but would warm feelings even make a dent first thing in the morning? I've tried for years to get my kids out of bed using gentle tones. It doesn't work. Sometimes sterner, more practical stuff is called for, especially early in the morning.

But move beyond the wording for a moment, and beyond memories of stiff rote recitations as you stood by your desk in a Catholic grammar school classroom. What's going on in this prayer?

When I look closely at this prayer, I see that, first of all, it grounds me. Like those fidgety seminarians, I need it. When I offer Jesus everything that happens to me today, I'm forcing myself to be aware of the endless potential for holiness that awaits me. There is nothing in this day that is going to happen apart from God, nothing that awaits me that is empty or worthless or useless. Even if it hurts, even if it's boring, God is present and can work through it.

The particular twist in this prayer though, is what all my "prayers, works, joys and sufferings" are for.

Every action, of course, has a multitude of dimensions, motives, and purposes. If my husband takes our fussy toddler out of my hair in that always delightful predinner hour, he does so for many reasons. He loves his son and wants to spend time with him, especially after a day in the presence of dull, frustrating adults at work. He wants to help Joseph feel better and perhaps educate him on the best arc for a falling basketball. He hopes to see my mood improve. And, of course, he would like dinner. Before the eleven o'clock news.

So it is with any of our actions. We do them for our own edification and pleasure, we want to help others, we want to pass the time. And while we're at it, we can also plug them into the mysterious reality of what God is doing in the world to reconcile it to himself (Colossians 2:15–20). We can, as we used to say, "offer it up."

It's a difficult concept to unpack, particularly in these times in which sacrifice is not exactly the hottest topic in religion. We are uncomfortable with the idea because it brings to mind the concept of a demanding God, always ready to judge and test us by how much we're willing to sacrifice.

You could take the Christian understanding of sacrifice and offering that way, I suppose. Many have in the past and still do. But you might be better off listening to what Paul said in his letter to the Romans as he redefined sacrifice for the new believers in Jesus:

> I urge you therefore, brothers, by the mercies of God, to offer your bodies as a living sacrifice, holy and pleasing to God, your spiritual worship. Do not conform yourselves to this age but be transformed by the renewal of your mind, that you may discern what is the will of God, what is good and pleasing and perfect. (Romans 12:1–2)

Sacrificing to God, then, offering our "prayers, works, joys and sufferings" means that the most important, foundational level of motivation in our lives is our love for God. "Offering it up" is an act of worship. It's a way for us to "pray without ceasing," as Paul exhorts elsewhere (1 Thessalonians 5:17). When we live as an offering to God, we're transforming ourselves and transforming our world.

I don't know exactly how it works, but I do know that a day in a world filled with people who have offered their daily actions up, so that God's will of love and justice be done, would look a lot different than one filled with people simply offering up their actions to the highest bidder.

The Morning Offering hooks me into reality first thing; the minute I wake up I am reminded that God will be present every moment of the coming hours. But it also ties me into a bigger reality, the reality of how God is working throughout the whole world to bring his children to him in love. What I do today is connected in a million ways to a bigger world, and this prayer plugs all of what I will do today into one more connection on the power strip.

Around the world today, people are praying, which means that people are putting their lives into God's hands. They are doing this when they say and participate in Mass; they are doing it when they chant Psalms or take ten seconds in gratitude or when, in the spirit of this prayer, they open mail, run a meeting, pick up kids, or stand vigil at a sickbed.

And a lot of them—those in the Apostleship of Prayer, or even those who just say this prayer because it means something to them—are doing so in conscious union with others, including the pope. You'll notice that the final part of the prayer concerns specific intentions of the entire church. At the beginning of every year, the Vatican really does issue lists of monthly intentions to be incorporated into this prayer. There are two categories: intentions for missionary activity, and general intentions for the church. It's just one more way of bringing us together in God's love. I'm not living for myself alone. I'm joined with an entire church, living for God's kingdom in all it does.

My life is a gift, and it's not a gift hidden in a closet for me to open on a better day. It's the gift of the here and now. An eighteenth-century French Jesuit named Jean Pierre de Caussade gave a series of spiritual conferences to the Visitation Sisters, from 1733 to 1740, on precisely this theme. The talks are collected in a volume called *The Sacrament of the Present Moment.* In it, de Caussade brings to us the power of the present that greets us every morning:

> The present moment holds infinite riches beyond your wildest dreams but you will only enjoy them to the extent of your faith and love. The more a soul loves, the more it longs, the more it hopes, the more it finds. The will of God is manifest in each moment, an immense ocean which the heart only fathoms in so far as it overflows with faith, trust and love.[2]

The Daily Offering confronts me with this gift of the present moment in all of its breadth and depth. Looking at the beauty and mystery that are my life, I have a choice: I can turn them over to God and his loving purpose, or I can turn them over to a world that will drain me dry as I wait in vain for its promises to come true—tomorrow.

salve.
regina

Hail, holy Queen, Mother of mercy,
Hail, our life, our sweetness and our hope.
To thee do we cry,
Poor banished children of Eve,
To thee do we send up our sighs,
Mourning and weeping
In this vale of tears.
Turn, then, most gracious advocate,
Thine eyes of mercy toward us;
And after this our exile,
Show unto us the blessed fruit
Of thy womb, Jesus.
O clement, O loving,
O sweet Virgin Mary!

The Prayer for Help

In the monastery on an island in the middle of a lake lived a man who couldn't move.

His name was Hermann, and the monastery had been his home since he was a child, since his aristocratic parents had sent him there to be raised and educated by Benedictine monks.

Such a decision—to put a child in the care of a monastery—wasn't uncommon in the eleventh century, even for children who weren't severely handicapped, as Hermann was. Abbeys and monasteries flourished in medieval Europe, providing centers of teaching, book preservation, art, and scientific inquiry for a culture slowly coming back to birth after the long Dark Ages. Unlike today, monastic life was not considered odd or unusual. Men interested in spirituality, education, an ordered life, and, yes, even power, filled monasteries and preserved and nourished the spiritual and intellectual life in Europe, as they welcomed travelers, tended the sick, educated youth, copied books, and advised secular rulers.

So it was quite normal for a family to place its son under the monks' care, and especially so if he needed the constant assistance that Hermann did, and especially if he showed the brilliance that Hermann did, even at the age of seven, when his parents sent him to the monks in the Abbey of Reichenau, on Lake Constance in Germany.

Hermann Contractus, Hermann of Reichenau, or, as he's known more commonly and less sensitively to modern ears, Hermann the Cripple, was barely able to move. His limbs were stiff and unyielding. His speech was slow and labored, and he could barely speak above a whisper. He could write, but only very slowly, so most of his thoughts were written down by a fellow monk acting as a scribe. Despite all this, Hermann managed to pack an amazing amount of achievement into his forty-one years of life.

He compiled one of the first chronicles of the history of the world since the life of Christ. He wrote one of the first geometry textbooks. He directed the construction of clocks, as well as musical and astronomical instruments. He was beloved as a teacher.[1]

And Hermann Contractus, in his room in his abbey on the island, wrote hymns.

One that survives a thousand years later, that was definitely written by him, is called *Alma Redemptoris Mater.* Another one that is frequently attributed to him, although without a hundred percent certainty, is *Salve Regina,* or as we know it in English, Hail, Holy Queen.

Hermann Contractus is one of four likely suspects for composing this hymn, and he's usually understood as the most likely because of the stronger documentary evidence linking him to its composition, as well as the fact that of the four, he is the only one who is definitely known to have composed hymns and prayers of this sort.

The evidence for Hermann is certainly stronger, for example, than that linking it to St. Bernard of Clairvaux. The legend there is that, in the middle of the night, Bernard heard voices coming from the monastery chapel. He followed the voices and found there the Virgin Mary, surrounded by angels singing the Salve Regina, which he then proceeded to learn by heart, wrote down, and sent to the pope. But even this is not a claim that Bernard composed the piece, merely that he heard it and passed it on.

History tells us that Hermann had a busy, quite fruitful life, and that he had strong faith. But the Salve Regina reflects the yearnings that even the most successful of us have to admit lie buried beneath our cheery surface, and that might particularly echo in the nighttime prayers of a seriously disabled man who was once a child left at an island monastery by his parents.

The Salve Regina became one of the most popular hymns of the succeeding centuries. Monastic communities adopted it and often gave it a special place after Compline, the last prayer of the day, right before bed. Cistercians, Dominicans, Carmelites, and Benedictines all spread its use throughout Europe. In 1444, a gathering of Benedictines explained its use after Compline:

> In order that the wily serpent may not beguile those in the
> night time whom he is unable to overthrow in their waking

hours, we think it necessary that before sleep we should implore her help who crushed the serpent's head.[2]

Outside of monasteries, the Salve Regina was used in processions, in the evening devotions from which many scholars believe Benediction of the Blessed Sacrament eventually developed.

And, most interesting, the song was used by mariners. Many of their accounts in the late Middle Ages and Renaissance attest to the use of the Salve Regina in services on ships at sea. Christopher Columbus mentions the Salve many times in his journals in entries such as this one, dated October 11, 1492, the day before he sighted the New World:

> When they said the *Salve,* which all the sailors are in the habit of saying and singing in their way, and they were all assembled together, the Admiral implored and admonished the men to guard the stern fore-castle well and to keep a good look out for land.[3]

The Salve was also one of the first prayers that the explorers taught the native peoples whom they encountered.

The Salve Regina is an appeal for help. We might wonder why we are asking Mary for this help, and think of it as some medieval pseudo-goddess worship. We'd be wrong to think that way, though.

First of all, appeals to Mary for her help did not begin in the Middle Ages. The oldest prayer that we have addressed to Mary is called the *Sub Tuum: We fly to your patronage, O holy Mother of God;*

despise not our petitions in our necessities but deliver us always from all dangers, O glorious and blessed Virgin. It dates from third-century Egypt, where documentary evidence indicates it was used in the Christian liturgies.[4] What is at work there, and in the Salve Regina, and in all Marian devotions, is the conviction that as the first disciple, as our sister and mother, Mary can pray for us.

Consider how Mary is addressed in the Salve Regina. All that we say about Mary is in the context of her relationship to Jesus. "Mother of mercy" doesn't mean that mercy, as a concept, comes from Mary. It means that Mary is the mother of *Jesus,* the seat of mercy.

In fact, there is only one specific request in this whole prayer: *Show unto us the blessed fruit of thy womb, Jesus.*

We've spent a lot of words in this prayer spilling out our woundedness, and it's clear what we're hoping to find: wholeness and peace. It's also clear where we expect to find it: in Jesus.

Over the years, the Salve Regina has been used in many settings, but it's the singing or praying of it at Compline that resonates the most.

After the chaos of a long day, families often look forward to the children's bedtime, and not just because they want some peace for themselves. No, there's something else about bedtime. At that time, there are stories and quiet conversations about the day that has just passed. There are prayers, and maybe even a little confession and forgiveness. There are assurances that all will be well, that the night holds no real terrors, and that tomorrow will be a chance to begin again.

We have all been there, at bedtime. We have been the parent, friend, aunt, uncle, or grandparent. We've been the babysitter. We have also—every one of us—been the child, brought home to rest in the arms of a mother. Deep within our memories, resonating still, that particular form of rest is how most of us leave one day behind and hope that tomorrow things will be better.

Along with the monks and nuns, along with the ordinary Christians praying their office or fingering the final bead on their rosaries, along with all those trying to make sense of weakness of body and spirit, trying to find hope—with all these we can turn to our Mother before we sleep, asking for a peaceful rest and a hopeful tomorrow, knowing that, in Jesus, it can be found.

the act of contrition

O my God, I am heartily sorry for having offended you, and I detest all my sins, because of your just punishments, but most of all because they offend you, my God, who are all good and deserving of all my love. I firmly resolve with the help of your grace, to sin no more and to avoid the near occasion of sin.

The Promise of Mercy

I find, more often than not, that comparing my relationship with God to my relationships with other human beings can be illuminating, often in a disturbing kind of way.

The teens I used to teach in Catholic high schools would sometimes take umbrage at these analogies. "How can you say that?" they'd demand. "God is so different from us."

Sure. But we're not different from us.

In other words, the analogy doesn't serve to expose God so much as it serves to expose us. Most of us, for example, accept the cold hard truth that you can never completely and totally understand another human being. You probably aren't endowed with perfect self-knowledge, either, come to think of it. Try to describe the person you love most in twenty-five words or less. It can't be done, and as much as it frustrates us at times, we accept it, and we respect the mystery of the human person, including ourselves. We still love despite the mystery, though, and perhaps even a little bit because of it. It tantalizes us and moves us to intimacy.

But God's a different story. For some people, if God's ways can't be explained in twenty-five words or less, if his being defies neat definitions, then this inability to understand God becomes an argument against his very existence.

So really, the issue isn't God's ineffability. It's our pride.

We can take the analogy even further, into relationships themselves. We all know that a good, deep, fruitful relationship of any kind takes time, energy, commitment, work, and communication. But our relationship with God is apparently just supposed to happen and flourish on the basis of an hour per week in church, plus one desperate plea for a traffic light to stay green on Thursday afternoon.

God comes to us as he is, but he also comes to us as we are, and, if for human beings, relationships are built on knowledge, communication, and commitment, and if those relationships take time to grow and mature, that's the way our relationship with God is going to be, too.

How do you feel when someone you care about, but who has hurt you, comes to you, says, "I'm sorry," but you can tell from her eyes and tight-lipped grimace that, while you know you're not supposed to judge, she obviously and clearly doesn't mean a word she's saying?

When my husband was in college, there was a guy who would regularly come into the residence deep in the night, banging doors as he made his way down the hall. Met with complaints, the guy would say "I'm sorry," in a tone that made it clear he was anything but.

So what good are the words if you really don't care about the other person's feelings, you're not particularly committed to changing your behavior, and the only reason you're apologizing is out of the faint hope that the person you ticked off won't spread the word through the office about what a witch you are?

And, if this attitude is not good enough for your spouse or best friend, how could it be good enough for God?

Most of us learned about the traditional Catholic sense of what it means to be sorry for sin, not through abstractions, but through internalizing a prayer we had to memorize and repeat—often in fear and trembling of forgetting the words—in the confessional. It's called the Act of Contrition. There are scads of versions of it out there, but the one at the beginning of this chapter captures the gist of all of them.

Despite the variations, all the versions of this prayer share an underlying structure of theological ideas, and we absorbed these ideas about sin and forgiveness without even knowing it, when we learned the prayer.

Quite simply, we learned that real sorrow for sin, or contrition, involves three points: being truly sorry; despising the sin because it violates our relationship with God, whom we love; and resolving not to sin again. It's all there in the prayer: what the theologians call perfect contrition.

And yes, there is imperfect contrition or, as it is also known, attrition. That's a sorrow for sin that is based more in fear—either of punishment or, it's interesting to note, of the damage that sin might do to you. If I'm unjustifiably harsh with one of my children, I will certainly be sorry about that, but why? What's my motivation for wanting to reconcile? Is my so-called "sorrow" for what I've done rooted in my love for God, the creator of these children's lives, who wants their happiness? Or does it come out of the fear that they might be trashing me in therapy twenty years down the road, or out of a desire to assuage my perpetual guilt over my maternal inadequacies?

But cheer up if you're imperfect like me. Theologians have always, always taught that imperfect contrition is good. It's not called "bad contrition" or "fake contrition," but merely "imperfect." It gets us to a better place than we were before. It opens our eyes and our hearts to forgiveness and healing. But it's through perfect contrition, rooted in the love for God above all else, that we really break, at a deeper level, the hold that sin has on us.

The Act of Contrition, known to most of us as a part of the sacrament of reconciliation, evolved over the centuries as a way for people to give expression to their contrition in an authentic, complete way. In older books it's often called the Act of Perfect Contrition because that's what it embodies.

There's a good chance that as many of us absorbed the Act of Contrition, we drank in a good dose of legalism as well, imagining that contrition involves one of the many checklists we've convinced ourselves God is keeping. It's easy to see this idea of perfect contrition in that way, but if we do, we ironically render the whole thing a hopeless conundrum: If we're perfectly contrite, we're sorry because we love God, so we'd better make sure we've fulfilled all the requirements for perfect contrition. Or else we won't be forgiven.

And unfortunately, that sort of legalistic thinking does, indeed, lurk in the background of the history and teaching of this prayer and those like it. But I'd like to try to turn that on its head and look at the Act of Contrition and everything it embodies as a gift rather than an obligation.

Quite simply, try reading the prayer again, and instead of hearing "must" behind every line, try hearing a promise.

When I think about what makes people miserable, myself included, high on the list are feelings of guilt and unresolved pain. "Issues," we like to call them these days. Our past sins press down on us, reshaping our sense of self. We may even start defining ourselves by our sins. We can't believe God would ever forgive us, so we just keep them to ourselves and let the guilt and regret grow. Jesus talked about lost sheep and forgiving fathers, but not for a minute do we really, deep down, believe that those words could be about us.

It is perhaps just for us that Paul wrote to the Romans: "For sin is not to have any power over you, since you are not under the law but under grace" (Romans 6:14). Paul is saying that because we are bound to Christ we are no longer defined by our sins. Our sins are forgiven, and we are free to be who God wants us to be: his own.

But it is so hard to believe that. The people we hurt die or move away beyond the reach of apologies. We witness the seeds of our past sins taking root and growing, even in the lives of others. We convince ourselves that because of what we have done, we simply don't deserve to be happy, so we will not try anymore.

The good news is that God pours out the forgiveness that makes real freedom possible through Jesus. Nothing is too terrible, no sin too distant in the past for mercy to reach. That is a promise. "[W]e must celebrate and rejoice . . . he was lost and has been found" (Luke 15:32).

But, doubters all, we find that whole scene a little hard to take. In a fit of pride and fear, we somehow imagine that our sins have the power to confound God. Who knows why we do it. But we do.

This is where contrition enters the picture. It is not an obligation but a promise to people who just don't want to believe that God loves them as much as he really does.

The Spirit tells us through the tradition of the church: You're sorry? Because you love God? Resolve to break free of that sin? There you go—now go in peace, really; put it behind you, and just trust in God's mercy. Stop carrying it with you.

What's interesting to me about this prayer is that we don't speak of "praying" it. We say that we "make an Act of Contrition," not that we say a prayer of sorrow. The difference is profound. These are not just words. And they are much more than a request. They are words attached to an internal act by which we deeply and completely, as much as we are able at that moment, open ourselves to God's mercy.

There are other acts in Catholic prayer. Most well-known are probably the acts of faith, hope, and charity focused on those three theological virtues that are the foundation of Christian life.

St. Peter Canisius, a great Jesuit educator and writer of the Counter-Reformation period, placed acts of faith, hope, and charity in his "Manual of Catholicism," and from that point, these prayers that began "I believe," I hope," and "I love" could be found in most Catholic catechisms and sometimes in the context of the Mass; they were recited and sometimes explained at the end of homilies.[1]

How can words be acts? Well, what else are they? An act, in traditional Catholic thinking, is a full expression of the will, free of ignorance, force, passion, fear, or habit. So certainly, saying "I love you" is an act of love. Telling someone "I believe in you" is an act of hope. Saying "I'm sorry" is an act of contrition, offered, not because we have to, but because in that act we find the gift of a gracious God: freedom.

the jesus prayer

Lord Jesus Christ, Son of God, have mercy on me a sinner.

Pray without Ceasing

This prayer is all about the air we breathe. It's about physically breathing, and it's about what keeps us alive, body and soul. If we don't breathe, we die.

Lord Jesus Christ, Son of God, have mercy on me a sinner.

This prayer is ancient, first appearing around the fifth century, but with roots in the New Testament. It's a foundation of Eastern Orthodox spirituality, but echoes and forms of it are found in Western Christian spirituality as well, in monastic prayer especially.

Its power, the tradition tells us, lies not only in the words, but in the mode of praying. The Jesus Prayer is not for praying once a day when you wake up or go to sleep or are fighting to control your temper. It's made for repetition and for letting the words burrow into our bodies and our lives as they are repeated hundreds of times a day, attached to the rhythm of breath that keeps us alive. We breathe in, we breathe out. We live. We pray *Lord Jesus Christ, Son of God*. We pray *Have mercy on me a sinner*. We live.

In his two letters to the Thessalonians, written to new Christians in Greece, Paul wrote about the hopes for Jesus' return and for those who died in the meantime. He wrote of moral questions, and near the end of the First Letter to the Thessalonians, as Paul ran down a list of qualities these Christians should nurture, he wrote: "Pray without ceasing" (1 Thessalonians 5:17).

And for centuries since, the question has irked us: How are we supposed to do that?

Most of us take the easier, nonliteral way out. Start off the morning dedicating everything you do to God. Give it all to him, maybe through that Morning Offering, and there you have it. Your day is a prayer, and you are, therefore, praying without ceasing.

And, who knows? That could be exactly what Paul meant. Live your life for God, and that, of course, is a prayer. But what if he didn't? What if he really meant, "Never stop praying"? "Pray all the time"?

That possibility is dramatized in a work—possibly fiction, possibly a spiritual memoir—that comes to us from an anonymous nineteenth-century Russian writer. Translated into English in 1930, *The Way of the Pilgrim* is the source for much of the modern interest in the Jesus Prayer.

The story is about a contemporary Job, a man who has lost everything, including his wife and the use of one of his arms. He decides to take to the road, wandering with nothing but a few crusts of bread and the Bible.

On his journey, he walks into a church and hears Paul's exhortation being proclaimed: "Pray without ceasing." The pilgrim puzzles over this and other Scripture passages that encourage frequent, if not constant, prayer. He searches for a teacher to explain all this to him, to no avail, until he happens upon a monk who introduces him to the Jesus Prayer, which seems to have emerged first in Eastern Christianity around the fifth century. The monk tells the pilgrim that once he has reached the point where he can pray the Jesus Prayer twelve thousand times a day, the kingdom of heaven will be within him.

And so the pilgrim follows these instructions, and the monk who gave them is dead by the time the pilgrim has worked up to twelve thousand repetitions in a single day. But when he reaches this goal, something mysterious and profound happens: his heart somehow takes over the prayer, and the prayer begins to live within him, which really means that it is Jesus who dwells there. Jesus is welcome, intimate, one with the pilgrim, and his presence overwhelms any physical suffering with joy so that, as one writer puts it, "his lips remain silent and all he has now to do is to listen to the heart speaking."[1]

A century or so later, American writer J. D. Salinger makes the Jesus Prayer a central trope of *Franny and Zooey:*

> "If you keep saying that prayer over and over again, you only have to just do it with your lips at first—then eventually what happens, the prayer becomes self-active. Something *happens* after a while. I don't know what but something happens, the words get synchronized with the person's heartbeats."[2]

Which is why the other name for this prayer is, most appropriately, the prayer of the heart.

Lord Jesus Christ, Son of God, have mercy on me a sinner, is what the pilgrim learned, repeated, and integrated into his life. The phrase is rooted in the parable of the Pharisee and the tax collector that's related in Luke 18:9–14. The Pharisee–the respected religious leader–stands and thanks God that he is not like other men, especially the tax collector. For his part, the tax collector will not even look up to heaven but can only beat his breast and say, "O God, be merciful to me, a sinner."

Other phrases can serve as the prayer of the heart as well, all cries to Jesus for the gift of what we most need: mercy. It's good to understand that mercy is more than just forgiveness for sins. In its fullest sense, it means generosity, or, quite simply, love–the deeply healing love that only God can give.

On the road, a blind man cried out, "Jesus, Son of David, have pity on me!" (Mark 10:47)

As Peter sank into the sea, he begged, "Lord, save me!" (Matthew 14:30)

St. Francis of Assisi was found in the middle of the night saying nothing but, "My God and my all!" over and over. Another account tells of him frequently drawing aside to repeat, "O God, be merciful to me the sinner!"[3]

Christians have used all of these phrases as prayers of the heart, and more: "My Jesus, mercy," St. Faustina's "Jesus, I trust in you," or even simply repeating the name, "Jesus" as the core of their prayer. Sometimes this prayer is repetitive and meditative, along the line of the Eastern Jesus Prayer, and sometimes it has a slightly different use, in what are traditionally called "aspirations" or "ejaculatory prayers," whereby the person simply speaks one of these phrases as a prayer, wherever he or she happens to be.

When St. Francis de Sales recommends this kind of prayer, he says, "The pilgrim who takes a little wine to restore his heart and refresh his mouth stops for a while but does not interrupt his journey by doing so. . . . pronounce either within your heart or with your lips such words as love suggests to you at the time."[4]

An interesting and actually rather charming variation of this prayer emerged in the sixteenth century. Composed by an Englishman, Richard Whitford, the Jesus Psalter is almost a combination of Western ejaculatory prayer and a certain amount of Eastern, rhythmic Jesus praying: "Jesus, Jesus, Jesus, I adore Thee. Jesus, Jesus, Jesus, I love Thee; Jesus, Jesus, Jesus have mercy upon sinners: Jesus, Jesus, Jesus, Thy Kingdom come . . ." and so on. It was popular because it was recommended for many: for the invalid, for those who must walk often on busy streets, for those afflicted with sleeplessness, and anyone who sought to pray without ceasing and live in the awareness of God's presence.[5]

In some ways, the traditional, repetitive, breathing-related Jesus Prayer of Eastern Christianity may seem to have something in common with Eastern, non-Christian ways of meditation involving mantras, but it's important to see the difference. We don't pray the Jesus Prayer in order to work ourselves into a meditative state or trance. After all, part of the purpose is to incorporate the prayer into every nook and cranny of our lives, and meditative trances usually aren't recommended when you're fighting traffic, in the middle of a meeting, or stirring a bubbling pot on a gas stove with a two-year-old threatening at the door.

No, the Jesus Prayer is an almost perfect reflection of the core and focus of Christian faith, for it is simply about Jesus. An optimal state of mind is not the primary goal of our faith; our real goal is a relationship with the living God, which is just where the Jesus Prayer takes us.

It takes us there first through the words. Just as with the Lord's Prayer, at the very beginning, we are oriented, we put our lives in the right relationship with Jesus. He is Lord. He is Son of God. As the late Russian Orthodox Metropolitan Anthony Bloom wrote of this prayer: "These words sum up all we know, all we believe about Jesus Christ, from the Old Testament to the New, and from the experience of the church through the ages. In these few words we make a complete and perfect profession of faith."[6]

We are uttering the name—the name which, Paul tells us in his letter to the Philippians, is above every other name and at which "every knee should bend" (Philippians 2:9–10). Jesus Christ is Lord. In Acts, Peter tells the Sanhedrin, "nor is there any other name under heaven given to the human race by which we are to be saved" (Acts 4:12).

The second part of the prayer brings us into the picture, exactly as we are and expressing exactly what we need. We are sinners, we are in need, and we are loved. We wouldn't ask unless we believed God would attend to our request, and by asking for mercy we are expressing our trust that God loves us.

So this is a good prayer to say even once in a while. But Christians have not been content with saying it once in a while. As *The Way of the Pilgrim* and Orthodox practice shows, the real fruit lies in the repetition.

Here is what happens, or can. When we repeat the name of Jesus and this prayer of our heart, we are letting the Incarnation be more than a concept, more than a doctrine. We're opening ourselves to its absolute reality. In Jesus, God entered into the world—which means our lives—in the most intimate way. That mercy is here, all the time, washing over us every moment, if only we could wake up and see.

When we repeat Jesus' name in prayer, we awaken. For ancient peoples, a person's name embodied the identity in a mysterious way. That's why Jews do not say or even write God's "proper name" (the name he revealed to Abraham), referring to him instead by other titles such as "Lord." Human beings could not see God and live, nor were they worthy of pronouncing his name.

In Jesus, though, the world has shifted. God has come down from the mountain, out of the clouds, and sat at our tables, touched us with his hands, given himself to us. In Jesus, we discover who God really is and who we really are, and not just on Sunday, but at every moment of the day, with every breath that we take.

As we say his name over and over and link it to our breath and to our heartbeat, we are opening our lives to him at the deepest level, and we can do that because that is what he did in the Incarnation. Our lives, joined with him through his name, become a prayer.

> When I arise in the morning, it starts me joyfully upon a new day. When I travel by air, land, or sea, it sings within my breast. When I stand up on a platform and face my listeners, it beats encouragement. When I gather my children around me, it murmurs a blessing. And at the end of a weary day, when I lay me down to rest, I give my heart over to Jesus . . . I sleep—but my heart as it beats prays on: "JESUS."[7]

One of the problems that many of us have in regard to prayer is that we're really busy. It's almost impossible to find a spare minute between breakfast and the last good night to brush our hair, much less take fifteen minutes to pray.

Although it's still important to find that fifteen minutes—or even five—alone with God, just as it's important to find a few moments alone every day with your spouse or child, the Jesus Prayer can help us find a way into intimacy with God in the midst of our organized chaos.

(And if you're wondering how those who try to pray the Jesus Prayer hundreds of times a day do so and keep track, know that the Orthodox use a knotted prayer rope, available at any Orthodox church, monastery, or bookstore. A rosary will do just fine, and there is even a special kind of prayer rope with a San Damiano Cross on the end that is used by Franciscans.)

The Jesus Prayer also helps us find peace, not only in the physical business of our day, but in the mental and spiritual cacophony as well. This is especially good if you have a vivid imagination and a short attention span, as I do.

Way too often, one of my two college-age sons calls and leaves a voice-mail message:

"Hey, Mom—can you call me?"

This kind of message, despite my pleas for more detail, is about the only kind they leave, and it drives me mad. These cryptic, uninformative messages have the power to send me into a panic, and immediately inspire a stream of imagined disasters.

And I can't stop worrying until I get in touch with them and hear the almost always ordinary purpose of the call: money, a question about one of their course readings, or money.

Our imaginations our powerful, and our intellects are, if not infinite in their powers, certainly rich with possibility. Our heads fill, our minds wander, we worry, we fantasize, we rationalize, we analyze, set off by anything and everything.

Busy minds, busy world. When I don't know what my sons want, my imagination creates horrid possibilities. When I don't know what the future holds for my life, my family, or my country, my mind can fill with all kinds of fearsome possibilities that hold me hostage. When I don't know why I'm here on earth, or have no sense of what life is all about, my imagination can go wild and, if I'm not careful, I can start living out what's in my imagination, possibly with disastrous results.

Untethered, with nothing or no one to trust in, unsure of what the truth is, my spirit flounders, and so do I. I can waste a lot of time thinking useless, pointless, directionless, or even destructive thoughts.

Or I can pray the Jesus Prayer.

Lord Jesus Christ, Son of God, have mercy on me a sinner.

anima
christi

Soul of Christ, sanctify me
Body of Christ, save me
Blood of Christ, inebriate me
Water from Christ's side, wash me
Passion of Christ, strengthen me
O good Jesus, hear me
Within Thy wounds hide me
Suffer me not to be separated from Thee
From the malicious enemy defend me
In the hour of my death call me
And bid me come unto Thee
That I may praise Thee with Thy saints
and with Thy angels
Forever and ever
Amen

Prayer for Happiness

Are you happy today? Were you happy yesterday? This morning?

Why?

We all want happiness; it seems that we are created to seek it. We may set our own terms for happiness differently—one person's heaven is another's hell, after all—but that general sense of contentment, satisfaction, and well-being is what we seem to be after. The ancients called it *beatus:* "blessed."

But what makes you happy? What brings it on? Go down the list. Here's mine, in all its shallow, shabby glory: my husband; my children, especially when they're fulfilling my plans for them; that moment at night when everyone goes to bed and I am finally alone; immersion in a good book, a good movie; absorption in the gifts of a composer, whether it be Beethoven or Lucinda Williams; that first taste of a caffeine-saturated beverage in the morning; finishing a piece of writing and getting ready for something new; seeing something novel and interesting; a beach; a mountain; a whispering snowfall at night.

Not as inspirational as someone else's list and not as decadent as another's.

But there's one thing for certain. Everything on that list—every single thing—is impermanent. So is the happiness it gives. One of the college-age sons can warm my heart today with interested questions about the *Aeneid* and frustrate me to anger tomorrow with admissions of skipping class. The CDs will wear out, and perhaps I will lose the ability to hear them. I may never see a beach or a mountain again. Guaranteed, in the end, everything will drift away, rot, or die, and what's also certain is that the happiness I get from a passing thing will pass. And then it will be my turn, along with everything else, to pass on. What will give me happiness then?

> Do not store up for yourselves treasures on earth, where moth and decay destroy, and thieves break in and steal. But store up treasures in heaven, where neither moth nor decay destroy, nor thieves break in and steal. For where your treasure is, there also will your heart be. (Matthew 6:19–21)

Or, as St. Augustine of Hippo wrote at the beginning of his *Confessions,* his account of his wandering way to Christ: "Our hearts are restless until they rest in You, O Lord."

There are times when we all need to know this. We've sought to ease the pain and fill the hunger with things that work for a while, then suddenly don't. Perhaps those things are even starting to hurt us. Perhaps the people we depend on to make us happy or to fulfill our lives, quite frankly, are tired of being asked to do a job that only God can do.

When this kind of subtle idolatry and useless activity threatens us, our relationship with God, and our true happiness, it's good to rest in the Anima Christi for a while.

Anima Christi, or "Soul of Christ," is one of those many prayers with shadowy origins. It's been attributed to a pope, a Franciscan, and the first Jesuit, but there's really no evidence that any of them wrote it. It just appeared in the fourteenth century in some diverse places: It's in the writings of a female Swabian visionary named Margaret Ebner; it's in several prayer books from around Europe; and, most intriguing, around 1364, it was inscribed over the door of a palace in Seville, Spain, a palace that had belonged to Moorish rulers for five hundred years and then was taken back in the reconquest.[1]

We find it also in a few late medieval liturgical instructions. Remember that, while the Mass maintained a basic, consistent structure throughout Western Catholicism at this time, there was still a great deal of diversity in ritual. We saw it with the various uses of the Lord's Prayer during the Mass, and it's true of Anima Christi, as well. In some places, it was said or sung during the elevation of the Host during the canon, or eucharistic prayer. In others, it occurs right before the Lamb of God, and it has consistently been a popular prayer to recite after communion.

But the prayer's strongest association is with St. Ignatius Loyola, the founder of the Society of Jesus, or Jesuit order, and one of the great Christian spiritual writers. Ignatius, a Spaniard, was a rather worldly soldier when he was very seriously wounded in a battle with the French and forced to spend many months in recuperation.

During that time, he read the Scriptures and read about the lives of the saints, and he experienced a total and complete conversion to Christ. He eventually formed, along with a small band of friends, the Society of Jesus. The members of this unique religious order, perhaps reflecting Ignatius's military background, committed themselves to the pope's service. The Jesuits quickly became known as a powerful force for education and missionary work in the post-Reformation world.

The core of Ignatius's spirituality is found in his *Spiritual Exercises,* a program of spiritual growth he wrote and revised many times during his life. Ideally, the *Exercises* are the foundation for a thirty-day retreat, but the insights and techniques can be helpful outside of that context as well.

The *Spiritual Exercises* is essentially a series of meditations and reflections centered on self-examination, with an ultimate goal of total openness to God. Ignatius emphasized use of the imagination in moving the participant through the recognition and rejection of sin and the embrace of glories of life with Christ. Toward this end, the exercitant, as one doing the Exercises is called, imagines him- or herself in the midst of various Gospel stories, being confronted with the reality of Jesus crucified, and even as a witness to the sufferings of those in hell.[2]

The primary goal of the *Exercises* is discernment. The meditations are intended to bring us face-to-face with reality: who we really are, the brutal fact of our own mortality, the hope of resurrection, and the very real call of Christ to each one of us. Through all this, self-deception and pride are drained away, in the hope that we might more clearly discern the voice of God in our lives and understand where he wants us to go from here.

The hope that Ignatius holds out is the same as Paul's when he writes, "[Y]et I live, no longer I, but Christ lives in me" (Galatians 2:20). The world, as good as it is, does not last. Only God is eternal, and when we immerse our entire selves in him, we are brought into eternity, as well, into a joy that never fades. It's an odd word that describes this stance: indifference. It doesn't mean that we don't care or that we lack empathy. In this context, indifference means a willingness to accept what comes, to find God in all things, and to live, no matter what, knowing that Christ loves us. Because of that, we can be blessed, *beata:* happy.

Ignatius recommends the use of the Anima Christi many times throughout the Exercises. In a way, it captures the essential spirit of Ignatius's wisdom, and it's easy to see why the prayer meant so much to him. It's not abstract in the least. The images are concrete and vivid. In the prayer, as in the Exercises, Christ is all. Christ is the one to whom we turn, who will give us all we need.

For when you read over the prayer, you find every human need expressed in its most basic form. We yearn to be sanctified—to be good. We hope to be saved—to preserve our lives. We may not want to be drunk (most of us), but we treasure feelings of giddy, complete, all-consuming joy. We want to be clean and strong; we want someone to listen to us; we want to be protected and safe.

Everything we do during the day that expresses our desire for happiness is, at some level, a desire for these things. Some of what we do takes us in that direction in a way that's helpful. Other things can quickly devolve into a waste of time: trying to feel connected to others only through the Internet, watching television for hours in the vain hope that something, at some point, will make us laugh. And others, such as addictive behaviors, sexual sin, and the pursuit of power and material goods no matter what the cost, are harmful.

Anima Christi brings us back to earth and points us to heaven. It reminds us that every earthly means will ultimately leave us hungry, and that every human connection, as holy as such connections can be, will eventually end. It reminds us of who will not fail us, whose joy is eternal, and who called himself living bread and water for a reason—because he is.

angel
prayers

Angel of God, my guardian dear, to whom his love commits me here. Ever this day be at my side; to light and guard, to rule and guide.

Holy Michael, the Archangel, defend us in the day of battle; be our safeguard against the wickedness and snares of the devil. May God rebuke him, we humbly pray; and do thou, prince of the heavenly host, by the power of God cast into hell Satan and all wicked spirits, who wander through the world seeking the ruin of souls.

Help in the Struggle

Angels enter our lives in childhood and, unlike some religious imagery, never really leave.

The culture won't let them, especially over the past few years when, perhaps befitting their identity, angels seemed to be everywhere: in Pulitzer prize-winning plays (*Angels in America*), in German films and their American remakes (*Wings of Desire* and *City of Angels*), in country songs ("Angels Among Us"). They flit about us with wings, on clouds, on plaques, pillows, and refrigerator magnets, in books, and on television programs, making everything right and dispensing greeting-card platitudes with California smiles.

The modern sense of angelic identity is a mix of a little bit of Christian understanding and a good dollop of wish fulfillment. Believe what you want about angels, but if you're coming at this from a Christian perspective, it might be good to start with the very basics of what we believe God has revealed about angels through Scripture. That, in itself, without any other pop culture fantasies, is plenty. Scripture tells us less than we want to know, more than we can imagine, and just what we need: The world is more than it appears to be. It has a purpose; we're part of it, and we're not alone.

The traditional prayers we address to angels hint at this. First, there's the little rhyme that a lot of us learned as children but hardly anyone knows the origin of: *Angel of God, my guardian dear, to whom his love commits me here. Ever this day be at my side; to light and guard, to rule and guide.*

The second most popular angel prayer is probably the Prayer to St. Michael, recited after Mass, along with other prayers, from the late nineteenth century to Vatican II:

> *Holy Michael, the Archangel, defend us in battle; be our safeguard against the wickedness and snares of the devil. May God rebuke him we humbly pray; and you, Prince of the heavenly host, by the power of God cast into hell Satan and all the evil spirits, who wander through the world seeking the ruin of souls.*

The imagery in these prayers is concrete and vivid, perhaps too vivid for some of us. But, underneath what some might see as excesses of piety, these prayers do point to truths about angels, truths taught by our tradition, which is always so careful to say enough but not too much about these messengers of God. Angels guide and protect human beings, not just because they're nice heavenly beings but because they are cooperating with God's will for our salvation.

Angel literally means "messenger": they are God's messengers, and they are all over the Bible, from the Garden of Eden, where they guard what is now shut off to human beings, to Revelation, where they join those at last redeemed in everlasting praise of God.

We learn from Psalms and Revelation that angels give glory to God through their praise. Angels brought news of miraculous births to Sarah, Zechariah, and Mary. Angels guided Joseph and the Magi. Angels ministered to Jesus in the desert. Angels met the women at the tomb and, as Jesus ascended to heaven, angels pointedly asked the apostles, "Men of Galilee, why are you standing there looking at the sky?"(Acts 1:11)

What we can discern from all of the stories about angels in Scripture is essentially this: They are spiritual beings with intellect and free will. They do God's work on earth, interacting with human beings, not manipulating them but most of the time simply communicating God's will. God has created a huge, complex world toward which he is anything but indifferent. He created it out of love, and all of his creation, as Paul tells us in Romans (8:18–23), is laboring toward fulfillment in God and a future of glory and peace that John lays out for us in particularly vivid imagery in Revelation (chapter 21). This is what the world is for. This is why we're here. Angels are a part of this creation and a part of this redemptive movement, the "unseen" part we speak of in the Nicene Creed.

A lot more has been said and written about angels. They've been named, described, and grouped in hierarchies. None of that is condemned by the church, but neither does any of it have absolute value or certainty. There are three angels named in Scripture, all of whose names in Hebrew are centered on God ("El"): Michael (Who is like God), Gabriel (My power is God) and Raphael (God heals). That is as far as official church teaching will go; that's as much as we think God has revealed to us for certain.

And note well what angels are *not:* They're not dead or pre-existent human beings. The Scriptures mention not a word about wings, clouds, harps, or haloes. They are unique beings who appear at your tent, asking for hospitality. They give you strange news. They praise God.

So why pray to angels? Why not just let them be? It's good to remember that our prayers to angels do not represent worship of angels. St. Augustine wrote that angels ". . . do not desire us to sacrifice to themselves, but to Him whose sacrifice they know themselves to be in common with us. For we and they together are the one City of God . . ."[1] We communicate with angels because we love them, as we love all of God's creatures, and because, as Scripture tells us, they're here to help us.

The idea of guardian angels—a specific angel assigned by God for each person—is not church doctrine by any means. It's suggested by Hebrews 1:14, which says of angels: "Are they not all ministering spirits sent to serve, for the sake of those who are to inherit salvation?" The idea was picked up by various early Christian thinkers, including St. Basil, who wrote in the fourth century quite explicitly: "Every one of the faithful has beside him an angel as tutor and pastor to lead him to life."[2]

The traditional prayer to the guardian angel, memorized by thousands of children and embroidered on hundreds of samplers through the years, expresses this conviction. Whether or not you believe in a personal guardian angel, this prayer points us to the truth that's revealed in Scripture: The world is made up of more than what we can see. And we are not alone. The guardian angel prayer resounds with the faith that God provides what we need to live in his peace. As adults we may not pray to guardian angels anymore, but perhaps reflecting on their presence can open our eyes to the possibility that God is working all around us, all the time, through all kinds of people and circumstances, to "light and guard, to rule and guide," if only we look.

St. Michael was the first angel to whom Christians gave particular attention and devotion. There's evidence that he was honored as early as the fourth century in Constantinople, as a healer. By the fifth century, he was being honored in Rome and subsequently in the rest of the Western Church, where he was seen primarily as the patron of soldiers. This view of Michael reflects his role in Scripture, especially in the vision in Revelation 12, in which Michael and his angels fought a mighty battle against Satan, who had taken the form of a dragon. The prayer to St. Michael, while not composed until much later, clearly reflects this role as protector.

While devotion to St. Michael is centuries old, this particular prayer to him dates only from the late nineteenth century. There's a legend, widely told but unsubstantiated, that Pope Leo XIII wrote this prayer after experiencing a terrifying vision of the fate awaiting the modern world. There's no credible source that affirms the truth of this story, but what is undoubtedly true is that the Prayer to St. Michael was written and put into its place in the liturgy (or, more precisely, after the liturgy) during Leo XIII's reign. Many Catholics who were formed in years before the Second Vatican Council learned the prayer in the context of the liturgy.

This prayer was one of what was called the Leonine prayers, a set of prayers recited by the priest and people after the final blessing, the point at which today we sing our recessional hymn and leave. For more than a century, though, this final blessing wasn't the end of Mass. The "final Gospel"—the first chapter of John—was proclaimed, and prayers were recited: three Hail Marys, the Salve Regina, some petitionary prayers, in some places what are called the Divine Praises, and this prayer to St. Michael.

Although this set of prayers was named for Leo XIII, most of these after-Mass prayers were added before Leo was pope. It was Pope Pius IX who first ordered a set of prayers recited after Mass as a special plea for God's protection of the Papal States (a big patch of Italy ruled by the pope for hundreds of years), which were slowly being stripped away from him by the forces of Italian unification. By the time Leo XIII came to the throne, the Papal States were gone (except for Vatican City), but other perceived threats to the church were out there, particularly the efforts in Germany to reduce the influence of the church in political, cultural, and social life. It's in this context that Leo added the Prayer of St. Michael. Even in this shorter version (there's a longer, more elaborate, even more vivid form), you can hear the defensiveness of a church that feels under siege.[3]

The prayer reflects an era in which the Catholic Church was in the midst of losing its comprehensive role in European culture, a process that perhaps began during the Reformation but was especially intense during the nineteenth century. During this time, European countries were racked with revolution and social change, and the church was usually perceived as the enemy of progress.

This vision of evil is perhaps not a sensibility that we can generally identify with these days, and that is undoubtedly a good thing. Evil exists and must be honestly identified and fought, to be sure. But for good or for ill, our commitment to do this is not so steeped in battle imagery as it was during the era that produced this prayer.

To be honest, though, don't we still experience that battle within? And if we raise our eyes to look outside of ourselves, we can certainly see forces that seek to demean and oppress God's children throughout the world. Evil is still here, and it's real.

When we contemplate these prayers to angels in the context of what we know about these spiritual beings, these messengers from God, we discern some truths about the way the world is. The existence of angels and their role in the universe as revealed through the Bible indicate that the world belongs to God and that he has a plan for it. He is working, mysteriously, to redeem this creation that he so loves.

Angels enter into human lives to assist us in discerning what that plan is, in embracing the plan, and in working with God to bring it to fulfillment.

The pop culture angel exists to help us achieve personal happiness. But the Judeo-Christian angel is about something bigger and more stunning: The angel of Christianity symbolizes the whole world as God has made it and as God is re-creating it, with our help.

When we pray these angel prayers, we are connecting with that process of re-creation. We're asking our guardian angel to guide us, not so that we can follow the world's path more successfully, but so that we can follow God's will more faithfully. At least that's supposed to be what we're doing. The Prayer to St. Michael connects us with God's plan in a specifically harsh way, but our reality does have harsh aspects, because evil exists. The Prayer to St. Michael assures us that God does not rest quietly while evil tries to rage.

And neither, in the company of angels, should we.

prayers of
st. francis

Lord, make me an instrument of your peace;
Where there is hatred let me sow love,
Where there is injury, pardon:
Where there is discord, unity;
Where there is error, truth;
Where there is doubt, faith;
Where there is despair, hope;
Where there is darkness, light;
Where there is sadness, joy.

O Divine Master, grant that I may not so much seek
To be consoled as to console;
To be understood as to understand;
To be loved as to love.
For it is in giving that we receive;

It is forgetting ourselves that we find ourselves;
It is in pardoning that we are pardoned;
And it is in dying that we are born to eternal life.

Most High, all-powerful, good Lord,
Yours are the praises, the glory, the honor, and all blessing.
To You alone, Most High, do they belong,
and no man is worthy to mention Your name.
Praised be You, my Lord, with all your creatures,
especially Sir Brother Sun,
Who is the day and through whom You give us light.
And he is beautiful and radiant with great splendor;
and bears a likeness of You, Most High One.
Praised by You, my Lord, through Sister Moon and the stars,
in heaven you formed them clear and precious and
    beautiful.
Praised be You, my Lord, through Brother Wind,
and through the air, cloudy and serene, and every kind of
    weather
through which You give sustenance to Your creatures.
Praised be You, my Lord, through Sister Water,
which is very useful and humble and precious and chaste.
Praised be You, my Lord, through Brother Fire,
through whom You light the night
and he is beautiful and playful and robust and strong.
Praised be You, my Lord, through our Sister Mother Earth,
who sustains and governs us,

and who produces varied fruits with colored flowers and
     herbs.
Praised be You, my Lord, through those who give pardon
     for
Your love
and bear infirmity and tribulation.
Blessed are those who endure in peace
for by You, Most High, they shall be crowned.
Praised be You, my Lord, through our Sister Bodily Death,
from whom no living man can escape.
Woe to those who die in mortal sin.
Blessed are those whom death will find in Your most holy
     will,
for the second death shall do them no harm.
Praise and bless my Lord and give Him thanks
and serve Him with great humility.

God in All Things

What saint, aside from the Virgin Mary, is more beloved than St. Francis of Assisi?

He stands among us, humble in his tattered brown robes, inviting us, and there's hardly a soul, Christian or not, who can turn away completely. Francis comes to us from across the centuries, talking of love, faithfulness, and peace. He watches our gardens. He stands in the front row of a Catholic school's All Saints' Day liturgy, a fourth-grade boy in a brown habit, complete with plastic birds perched on his shoulders, with an unidentifiable pope on his left and a nameless Roman martyr on his right.

St. Francis appeals to us because he testifies to possibilities. We listen to the gospel, and while it inspires us it also discourages and even frightens us. How can we possibly do this? Trust in God for our needs? Turn from even our families to God alone? Live like the birds in the field? Lose ourselves and live completely for others?

And even if we tried to do all of that, would it make us happy? We can't conceive of happiness without the stuff our culture swears will make us happy, and despite the cold fact that this stuff has let us down again and again, we can't quite believe that leaving it all behind would really give us peace. We are ordered, again and again, to find fulfillment and "bliss" and to just keep thinking more and more about ourselves in order to find them. Jesus promises that if that's our angle, we will not find fulfillment. "The last will be first" (Matthew 19:30). "Whoever finds his life will lose it" (Matthew 10:39). "Blessed are they who mourn" (Matthew 5:4).

Francis stands in witness, quite simply, to the truth of the gospel. Yes, it can be done, and yes it will give you peace, which is what happiness is really about.

So when we're struggling with this paradox and the extraordinary pressures from within and without to just give in and throw ourselves into things, money, and power, we turn to God for strength, and we often do this through St. Francis. It's like turning to a friend who's endured great loss when it suddenly becomes our turn to face loss. We remember her witness, we recall her words and her example, and if she's around, we give her a call and ask her for help. When we're struggling to live the gospel in a world of gorgeous, empty promises, St. Francis is that friend for many of us.

One of the prayers that express the possibilities that St. Francis embodies is the Prayer of St. Francis, or the Peace Prayer.

The most recent scholarship indicates that St. Francis of Assisi could not have written this prayer. The earliest mention we can find of the Peace Prayer appeared in a French religious journal in 1913, about 800 years after St. Francis lived. This journal gives as its source another journal, no longer in existence. The next appearances come from both Italian and French newspapers in

1916, saying that Pope Benedict XV had been sent a copy of the prayer, courtesy of yet another French periodical, crucial copies of which do not seem to exist and which are assumed to have been lost in one of the two World Wars. These earliest versions of the prayer, as printed in these newspapers and journals, make no mention of St. Francis or the Franciscans.[1]

The Peace Prayer came into wider circulation just a couple of years later on a prayer card printed for Third Order, or Secular Franciscans who were living in the region of Reims, France. Secular Franciscans live in the Franciscan spirit, take certain vows, but live in regular society rather than in community. On one side of the card was a picture of St. Francis, and on the other side was the prayer, called "Prayer for Peace," with an admonition that all Secular Franciscans live by the spirit of this prayer.[2]

From there, it popped up throughout Europe; for instance, it was adopted as the official prayer for the Christian Movement for Peace, which grew in Switzerland in the 1920s. The Reformed Church of France incorporated the prayer into its liturgy.[3] It's in a prayer book printed to accompany devotionals broadcast on the BBC in 1936.[4] After World War II, its popularity understandably grew, and it appeared in many different German and English prayer books after the war.

The earliest versions of this prayer attribute it to *Souvenir Normand,* that disappeared periodical. As the years went on, some versions added "attributed to St. Francis." This byline eventually won out, and from that point, the assumption was widespread that St. Francis was the author.

While the prayer is certainly in the spirit of St. Francis and the Gospels, it's not found in any of his writings or the early writings about him (of which there are actually quite a few). The prayer is more similar to some sayings of Blessed Giles of Assisi, one of Francis' early followers; a collection of his works was often included in French translations of *The Little Flowers of St. Francis,* beginning in the mid-nineteenth century:

> Blessed is he who truly loves and does not wish to be loved; blessed is he who fears and does not wish to be feared; blessed is he who serves and does not wish to be served; blessed is he who conducts himself well towards others and does not wish others to conduct themselves well toward him.[5]

It's not so important that Francis of Assisi did not write the Prayer of St. Francis, because it most certainly is in keeping with his spirit. And the people who first disseminated it were Franciscans. They, of all people, should recognize the words that express the essence of their founder's vision. This prayer asks for the grace to be able to live as Jesus did, and this aim was at the center of Francis's life.

We do, however, know of another prayer that was definitely written by St. Francis. We know it by a number of titles: The Canticle of the Creator; The Canticle of Brother Sun, Sister Moon; or, most popularly, The Canticle of the Sun.

According to one collection of stories, stories that can be dated back within a hundred years of Francis' life, the Canticle of the Sun was composed in three stages, all within the last two years of Francis's life.

In the popular mind, Francis is a carefree spirit wandering the fields outside Assisi accompanied by other equally carefree spirits. The real picture is a bit more complicated.

Francis experienced a total conversion to Christ, abandoning his life as the son of a wealthy textile merchant for radical gospel poverty. His initial call, as he experienced it from Jesus, was to "rebuild my church," which he took literally at first; initially he worked alone, and then later with a slowly growing band of brothers to reconstruct an abandoned chapel in San Damiano.

The real meaning of the call, though, became clearer as the years went on. Francis's path was to follow Jesus and to live the gospel in the most literal, simple way: possessing nothing; serving the poor, the sick, and the abandoned; and doing all this in the context of a life immersed in prayer and praise.

As so often happens, as the religious order grew, things changed, and not, in Francis's opinion, for the better. The radical vision was mitigated and then abandoned, and Franciscans in many places became as learned, secure, and settled as any other, more established, religious order. Francis himself resigned the leadership of the order, left the Franciscans to God, and spent the last few years of his life in contemplation. He also did some preaching, and struggled tremendously with increasingly poor health, especially with eye problems.

It's in this context that we need to see the Canticle of the Creator. According to tradition, the first part was composed around 1225, when Francis was living in near blindness, in wretched conditions and surrounded by hordes of mice. His order having grown beyond him, Francis may not have been near despair, but he was certainly wondering if his life had turned out as it was supposed to.

While in prayer one night, he received a rush of reassurance: "[B]e glad and joyful in the midst of your infirmities and tribulations: as of now, live in peace as if you were already sharing my kingdom."[6]

His grateful response was the first part of the Canticle of the Creator, which he then sent several friars out to sing as "true jongleurs of God" for anyone who would listen.[7]

The second part was composed in response to a dispute between the mayor and the bishop of Assisi. Francis heard about this dispute, which had so far resulted in the excommunication of the mayor and his subsequent order that no townspeople do business with the bishop. Francis asked that the two men be brought together, and that two friars stand before them and sing the Canticle with the added verses about peace and forgiveness. It worked.[8]

The final part, alluding to Sister Death, was added as Francis lay dying, while two brothers, Brother Angelo and Brother Leo, sang the Canticle to him, and, at his request, added the stanzas to praise and welcome Sister Death, for as Francis believed, she is the way to eternal life, and she does no harm to those who have faith.[9]

When we pray the Canticle of the Sun, we're praying along with St. Francis, this man who lived out the possibilities of the gospel—its joy and its pain. Francis understood that the world belongs to God and that when we look closely enough, we can see God's handprints through his creation. We see beauty, glory, and care.

Through this creation we can also see the qualities we are called to embody. We are called to be creatures, like the moon, stars, wind, water, fire, and earth, which are called to reflect glory and beauty, to provide sustenance to others, to be humble, chaste, playful, strong, and fruitful.

St. Francis is celebrated for his intimacy with nature, but it's important to remember that what he revered was not nature for its own sake but as a gorgeous reflection of God, as an amazing expression of God's generosity, love, glory, and care. St. Francis didn't worship nature. He worshiped God, and his worship of God evoked honor for what God had made and for what nature tells us about God.

The second and third parts of the prayer bring us to the heart of Francis's life: his faithfulness to Christ. Francis's conversion was not to a general sense of affection for humanity or to faith in an amorphous God. It was to Jesus Christ, Son of God. Jesus called Francis to follow him, and following him meant holiness and sacrificial love—the love evoked by the second part of the prayer, in which those who forgive, suffer, and live in peace are blessed. The blessedness comes, of course, when we meet Sister Death. The first death alluded to is, of course, the death to self we embrace when we come to Christ; and the second death is our bodily death, which, if we have been faithful, will do us no harm.

The question is, of course, when do we praise God? My first instinct is to offer praise when everything is going well. My oldest son calls, reporting that he made it home safely after his Christmas visit. My father's lungs are clear of cancer—this year at least. My husband sits beside me, holding my hand. So I utter thanks and offer praise, and when I look out on a perfect night from my safe, healthy life, I join with Brother Sun and Sister Moon and reflect on God's glory.

But I also know that this is only a part of life. Suffering has come my way before, and it will come again. Forgiveness will be hard but necessary, and peace might seem to hide behind impenetrable walls of conflict and pain. Francis wrote his Canticle, offering deep and authentic praise to God while he endured bodily suffering and earthly discouragement. Perhaps that is the power of this prayer—connecting us to God's love and glory in the midst of what the world calls misery.

Francis is a saint and an exemplar of faithfulness to Christ on a path that hardly any of us chooses to take. Despite his extraordinary holiness, each of us still has more in common with him than we think. No matter how far above us he seems, the truth is that we all will, to some extent, have to live like Francis, because we all are human, and we all will suffer.

The question is—will we be able to pray like him?

st. patrick's breastplate

Christ with me, Christ before me,
Christ behind me, Christ in me,
Christ beneath me, Christ above me,
Christ on my right, Christ on my left,
Christ in breadth, Christ in length,
Christ in height
Christ in the mouth of everyone who speaks to me,
Christ in the heart of everyone who thinks of me,
Christ in every eye that sees me,
Christ in every ear that hears me.
I arise today
Through a mighty strength, the invocation of the Trinity,
Through belief in the Threeness,
Through confession of the Oneness,
Of the Creator of Creation.

Prayer for Protection

Is this your life?

Ridiculous traffic on the way to work. Ridiculous people with ridiculous demands at work. Voices on the radio and talking heads on television continually presenting you with firm evidence of a world gone mad. Not enough time to do anything. So much need here, there, and across the world, and it's just you here wanting to help but not sure how. Relationships that you can never get quite right, children who won't stop worrying you. Temptation. Weakness. A quick glance at a cemetery as you speed by on your way to somewhere else, eyes averted, subject changed, radio turned up louder.

As Christians, we believe that life is marvelous, enchanting, and joyous. But it's also really hard, sad, and painful. And for each of us, in the end is that cemetery, no matter how many miles a day we jog, no matter how many nutritional supplements we take.

Aside from that basic instinct to survive, what can give us the strength to meet each day with joy?

Well, faith gives us strength. And I mean faith that is more than a general sense of hoping for the best or a belief that everything will come out all right in the end. Rather, I mean a specifically grounded faith that God is absolutely real. God created the world, including me, and God created me out of love. Every moment of every day, God is with me, listening, strengthening, comforting, guiding. And at the end, God will be waiting.

Christians have embraced a number of images to express their faith in God's support and protection. In Psalms 36, 63, and 91, the psalmist writes of finding safety under the shelter of God's "wings." In other psalms God is a fortress and a stronghold. Jesus tells us that we can expect God to protect and care for us as a shepherd cares for his sheep.

And since life is, in many ways, like a battle—a battle with external forces of wrong, and an intense internal battle within each of our souls—it's not surprising that God's power to protect those who seek him would often be compared to battle armor.

This imagery is all over the Hebrew Scriptures, as when the psalmist declares that "the Lord is . . . my shield" (Psalms 28:7). In his letter to the Ephesians, Paul draws on this ancient metaphor and uses it to give courage and strength to these new followers of Jesus who are seeking to be faithful to him in a hostile world:

> Finally, draw your strength from the Lord and from his mighty power. Put on the armor of God so that you may be able to stand firm against the tactics of the devil. For our struggle is not with flesh and blood but with the principalities, with the powers, with the world rulers of this present darkness, with the evil spirits in the heavens. Therefore, put on the armor of God, that you may be able to resist on the evil day and, having done everything, to hold your ground. So stand fast with your loins girded in truth, clothed with righteousness as a breastplate, and your feet shod in readiness for the gospel of peace. In all circumstances, hold faith as a shield, to quench all [the] flaming arrows of the evil

one. And take the helmet of salvation and the sword of the Spirit, which is the word of God. (Ephesians 6:10–17)

Picking up on this imagery is an ancient prayer which, according to tradition, is rooted in the life of one of our most beloved saints. It's called The Breastplate of St. Patrick, or the Lorica, or even The Deer's Cry, for reasons that will become clear in a moment.

Now, we don't know if St. Patrick actually wrote this prayer. Some scholars say he definitely did not, but others say that we can't be so sure. We do have two pieces of writing that can definitely be traced to St. Patrick—his *Confessions,* and *Letter to Coroticus* (in which he denounces the slave trade)—so it's not unimaginable that this could have survived, although the earliest manuscripts we have containing it come from the seventh century, two hundred years after St. Patrick lived and died.

But whatever the exact origins, there's no doubt that for thirteen hundred years (stop and think about that: *thirteen hundred years*) St. Patrick's Breastplate has been prayed and sung as a truthful expression of the profoundly Catholic spirituality that Patrick brought to Ireland and as an apt reflection of what we know about the faith that energized him. This prayer is suffused with a knowing confidence, knowledgeable and realistic about what awaits us in the world, and confident in God's desire and ability to protect us.

It is hard to imagine that Patrick, given the hardships of his life, could be anything but realistic. He was born, son of a deacon and grandson of a priest, perhaps in what we now call England, or some suggest, Scotland. What we do know is that as a teenager Patrick was kidnapped and taken to Ireland, where he lived as a slave for six years. He escaped back to Britain, and some scholars suggest that he traveled to Gaul, or modern France, where he studied and was ordained, but this is not certain by any means.[1]

Eventually he did return to Ireland to evangelize a place where Christianity had been planted but never really taken root, and where paganism still reigned among the Celts. So Patrick returned to this land where he had endured such suffering, to the people who had kidnapped him and killed other members of his family. He returned because he was called—in a vision, it is said, a vision in which voices cried out, "Come back and walk once more among us."

And so Patrick returned to preach the Good News and to walk among a people he knew full well would be hostile—and they were. He was imprisoned twelve times, did battle with Druid priests and kings, and fought widespread superstition. But just as deeply as he knew the danger, he knew the need. Who would know better a people's deep need for Christ than one who'd been kept as a slave among them?

According to legend, St. Patrick's Breastplate has its roots in one of these conflicts. A certain king named Laoghaire had invited Patrick to come and see him, planning, of course, to dispense of him along the way. He had soldiers stationed along the road ready to strike, but as Patrick approached with his band of followers, he began to pray the words of the Breastplate. As he prayed, darkness fell, and what the soldiers saw passing was no group of men but a line of deer, and all they could hear was a strange, music-like cry of the deer as they passed.

Called forth by Patrick's prayer, God's protection descended in the dark, like a *lorica,* the Celts said. A *lorica* was both a piece of armor and a powerfully protective charm. The protection enveloped them and let them be seen as deer, an animal sacred to the Celts, a symbol of power and life. The psalmist tells us that the deer longs for running water as we yearn for God (Psalm 42).[2]

Often, when we feel the need for God's protection and help through difficulty, we can say little more than "help!" This is perfectly fine and good because it comes from the depth of our need and is very much an expression of faith–we don't ask for help from people unless we know they can give it.

But it can be helpful, too, to turn to the words of an ancient prayer that carries the same sentiment. Patrick's prayer allows us to go beyond what our circumstances and emotions tell us to what God can provide for us: *Christ with me . . . Christ before me . . . Christ behind me . . . Christ in every eye that sees me, Christ in every ear that hears me . . .*

In the complete version of the prayer-poem, which is much longer, there are also ample references to the world around us, the expression of a time when human beings knew they were a part of nature, not above it, that all of it rested under God's hand: *I arise today through the strength of heaven: light of sun, radiance of moon, splendor of fire, speed of lightening, swiftness of wind, depth of sea, stability of earth, firmness of rock.*[3]

It seems that God's protection does not involve taking us away from the things of this world. God's support does not help us escape from our lives' difficulties. As Patrick's life shows in blazing color, it's the exact opposite. God doesn't call us to escape. In fact, our pain and suffering indicate to us where the Good News is most needed. We can go to that place of suffering because, on the cross, Jesus went there too.

When we pray St. Patrick's Breastplate, we are finding the breadth and depth of the strength that our loving God offers. We see that we are not, as we are so often tempted to think, alone. The words of protection still ring true because life itself teaches us that we need to hear them.

memorare

Remember, most loving Virgin Mary,
    never was it heard
    that anyone who turned to you for help
    was left unaided.
Inspired by this confidence
    though burdened by my sins,
I run to your protection
    for you are my mother.
Mother of the Word of God,
    do not despise my words of pleading
    but be merciful and hear my prayer.
    Amen.

The Mother Who Will Never Let Us Down

Encountering God directly sounds fantastic, but it's an open question whether most of us could manage it on a regular basis, or even weather the experience once and still get dinner on the table on time.

God is so great and we are so small, and God himself told Moses that no one could see his face and live. Job, questioning boldly, may have gotten close, yet even there, God addressed him "out of the storm" and the answer he gave to Job's question of suffering was, "Where were you when I founded the earth?" (Job 38:1, 4). Such a question seems to emphasize the distance between God and humanity.

But there's more to this apparent distance than our puniness, for God has reached out to overcome that problem. Jesus speaks our language, walks beside us, and shares our suffering.

The other issue is baggage, all the heavy, tattered, checked, lost, and reclaimed baggage of being human. God is pure spirit; we're not. Every encounter we have is mediated through a thousand different channels. It's mediated through our senses, our understanding, our personal histories, and our cultures.

In other words, God certainly may be yelling at us, but just think of all the walls his voice has to penetrate, all the tunnels, all the checkpoints it has to pass. If you've tried to reason with a tight-lipped teenager who is devoted to the notion that nothing you say could ever be right, you understand what I mean.

Is the fact that we reach out to God through our bodies and all that comes with them a negative? Well, sort of, and the goal of serious mystics is to strip away all the baggage of corporeality and be totally present to God as we are, as God is.

But on the other hand, it's the way we're made, and since God made us, he must have made provisions and perhaps even worked some kind of satisfying beauty into the whole thing, especially for us non-mystics. Perhaps there's something in the baggage, something in our particular embodiment and histories that can function not so much as a wall but as a prism.

This is really the whole idea behind the richness of the Catholic sacramental sensibility that over the centuries has permeated almost every corner of human experience and showed how we can find God there. Water, wine, bread, music, philosophy, sexuality, politics, and art—God reaches out to us through all these things and more, including other human beings.

So we find God through loving others and being loved. We turn to others and ask them to help us. We tell them that we're open to what God's love can accomplish through them as they listen, support, and pray for us, whether they are alive or with God. It's called the communion of saints.

First among the saints is Mary, the mother of Jesus, and the prayers asking for her help are too many to count, from every culture and age, each more flowery than the next. To some modern ears, these prayers can seem unnecessary or worse, a touch blasphemous. Go directly to God, we think. Do not pass go. Why ask Mary when God's right there?

Well–why ask anyone to pray for you? I suppose that's the question. Why pray for anyone else? Just let God handle it. He doesn't need your help. Or does he?

Aside from the Hail Mary, probably one of the most well-known prayers asking for Mary's intercession is the Memorare.

As is the case with most of our prayers, we don't know exactly who wrote this, or when. We find longer versions of the Memorare in early medieval Eastern Christianity, but the first time we find it popping up in anything close to this form is much later, in the seventeenth century.

For a long time, some attributed this prayer to St. Bernard of Clairvaux, a twelfth-century mystic and preacher who had a deep, passionate devotion to Mary. If you read some of his homilies, you hear some echoes of the Memorare, but never the exact form.

The confusion about Bernard undoubtedly occurred because it was another Bernard who vigorously promoted the use of the Memorare, and with whom it became closely associated: a fellow named Claude Bernard, a French priest who ministered to the poor and to prisoners.

He was called the "Poor Priest," and he lived from 1588 to 1641. He described his devotion to the Memorare in a letter to Anne of Austria, queen of French King Louis XIII. He had fallen quite ill and at some point prayed the Memorare, which he had learned from his own father. He was cured, but, as he said, "As I could not persuade myself that God had worked a miracle in my favour, I attributed the cure to some natural cause."[1]

He was soon set straight, though, when at the very moment he was speaking of his recovery to a friend, an Augustinian brother whom he hardly knew appeared at his door and told Bernard that Mary had appeared to him the previous night, told him that she had effected Bernard's cure, and wanted this brother to go and confirm this to Bernard.

Bernard got the message. From that moment on, the Memorare was Claude Bernard's prayer. His ministry was to the most hardened criminals, many of them condemned to die, and Bernard's biographers relate story after story of the prayer's importance in conversions, even on the scaffold—Bernard once climbed right up on a hangman's scaffold to try, one last time, to touch the heart of a criminal who'd rebuffed him many times before. The man pushed him off the platform onto the ground. Bernard climbed to his knees and started praying the Memorare. Finally moved, the condemned man asked to make his final confession.

Bernard got his prayer heard—or consumed, if that's what it took. Another criminal was due to be tortured and broken on the wheel. Unrepentant, he refused to pray with Bernard, who responded, "Well, since you won't say it, you shall eat it," and he promptly crammed a copy of the prayer into the man's mouth. Again, it worked. The condemned died, but not before he'd reconciled himself to God.

On his deathbed, the Poor Priest asked that he be given a crucifix and a copy of the Memorare, two hundred thousand copies of which he had printed up and distributed during his lifetime, "that he might press them to his lips and to his heart as the principal instruments of the work by which he had tried to serve his Master."[2]

> After his death, engraved portraits of Claude Bernard—who, by the way, has not even been beatified by the church—were printed and distributed, with the Memorare printed under his picture and with the heading "Oraison du R. P. Bernard A la Vierge" (Prayer of R. P. Bernard to the Virgin). It's easy to see how from this point, later printers might have carelessly begun attributing this prayer to the authorship of St. Bernard of Clairvaux. The earliest English versions appear in the very popular and widely used "Penny Catechism" in England in the early twentieth century, attributed to St. Bernard of Clairvaux.[3]

Now, this prayer and the way Claude Bernard used it may seem magical. Recite the words and be converted. Is that all it takes, a formula? Is that what this is about?

I don't think so, and I don't think Claude Bernard thought so either. I think the point of all of these stories about the Poor Priest and the Memorare is simply what it takes for some people to let God in.

We so often associate devotion to Mary with sweetness and sugary sentimentality, with retro, outdated images of femininity and motherhood. But you might have noticed that the stories of Claude Bernard's use of the Memorare are anything but sweetness and light. Claude Bernard ministered to people who had killed, had wrecked lives, including their own, and were facing death—and who were sometimes tortured beforehand—from a dark, hopeless, place. And nothing, not even the gallows, opened them to the fact that God might have something different, something better in store.

Until the Poor Priest threw himself on the ground and started praying the Memorare or stuffing it in their mouths.

It is just a fact of life that God is hard to fathom, and the further we push God away, the more difficult it becomes. Like a kid buried so deep in lies he can't look his parents in the face, like a couple whose relationship is so defined by externals, whose biggest fear is actually having to be alone together and having to talk, we can be so buried in our own baggage that God's voice is nothing but the faintest echo.

We need an intervention. We need mediation. We need someone we trust, someone who has something in common with us, to help us see ourselves as we really are and for what we could be. The deceitful kid needs to hear from someone who told the truth to his parents and lived to tell the story. The couple needs a smart-aleck daughter or a quietly observant friend to say, "Why did you guys get married, anyway?"

And the hardened criminal might just need a mother.

Looking at it from the other end, we don't just need others to help us open our eyes, we need them to help us work things out. We need another person in the room who can help us see with different, more objective eyes, who can help us see possibilities and hope to which we are otherwise blind.

So the hardened criminal can't see his own worth. But most of the time, and in a unique, primal way that begins in dark, damp silence with the steady rhythm of a beating heart, he knows that a mother can.

This is the way we are. This is the way we're built. We get lost in our own, often flawed, sense of reality. We close ourselves off. We can know truth, including the truth of God's love, only through who we are: in this case, men and women who are all children of mothers.

Is it so impossible that God would take note of this and let us come to him, when we need to, through a mother?

This may seem wrong to us, and it may violate our rational expectations of approaching God. But what it doesn't violate is our human nature. What's true is that devotion to Mary, and prayers like this, flowered during the Middle Ages, when God ruled in popular piety as a monarch and a judge, as fearsome as the lord of the manor who held the power over life and death. When people were starving for a hint of gentle mercy from on high, the role of Mary grew, not as an alternate god, but as an almost intuitive mass response to a truth. God *is* merciful. God *is* love. It will spill out somehow. We will find it somehow, even if we have to see it reflected off of someone else.

Of course, this is not just about Mary. We all are, in the end, called to mediate God's love and mercy for each other. When we need help, most of us don't just sit in a room and ask God for it directly. We run to our best friend, to our parent, to our spouse, seeking support, prayers, and a sympathetic ear. In the broadest sense, that is what church is—a body of people letting Christ love through them. And Mary, as the first member of the church, the one who said yes to God in faith, is the friend, the support, the mother we know we can always look to and who will, as this prayer says, never let us down. Others might forget to pray for us. She won't.

This prayer emerged during a period in the church's history when too many people, unfortunately, felt too distant from God, so they turned to someone who seemed to embody his love and mercy in a more approachable way. It's too bad, I suppose, and it's not ideal. But have things really changed so much? Do none of us ever feel distant from God, mystified by him, unsure of what he thinks of us, unconvinced that he could ever love us again?

People—especially men, oddly enough—have for centuries prayed the Memorare and found an answer, found the words moving them to suddenly, inexplicably open up to God's mercy. That mercy was real but hidden deep in their baggage of sin and shame; they found it by opening themselves to a mother.

God works, as they say, in mysterious ways.

suscipe

Take Lord, and receive all my liberty, my memory, my understanding, and my entire will, all that I have and possess. Thou hast given all to me. To Thee, O lord, I return it. All is Thine, dispose of it wholly according to Thy will. Give me Thy love and thy grace, for this is sufficient for me.

The Radical Prayer

Today, I took my son and daughter to a celebration of apples in a nearby small town.

It was a pioneer-day sort of affair, with cloggers, dulcimer players, men stirring ham and beans with long wooden paddles in big black pots, a black sheep looking resentfully out at an audience gathered around to gawk at his denuding, and of course, on this brisk October day in northern Indiana, apple dumplings, apple fritters, apple pie, and even apple burgers.

In one of the tents, two older ladies in calico and bonnets were running a game. Sawdust an inch deep was spread over the floor. Baskets filled with toys ringed the sawdust. Each child was to dig through the sawdust until he unearthed a flat wooden painted apple. Having found the apple, he could pick out a prize from the basket.

Well, little Joseph scraped through the sawdust, obviously overjoyed to be able to mess around with things on the ground without having them snatched out of his hand. After a couple of minutes, he found his apple. He obediently handed it to the lady in the bonnet and walked down the row of baskets.

And back up. And down. Taking this little wooden wagon, putting it back, picking up that feather headdress, putting it back. Up and down again.

Finally, it was all too much. He turned, threw himself back on the ground, and started scratching through the sawdust again. Too many choices had overwhelmed him. Give the boy one job, one goal. He can handle that fine.

I can sympathize.

Decision making can be like that. We may live in a time and place that allows us much freedom and choice, but there are times when we probably feel like Joseph. Too many choices. Too much freedom. We might as well trudge down the road more traveled; might as well watch the same channel out of two hundred every night; might as well keep sending our kids to the same lousy school even though we know it's lousy; might as well keep going to the same dreadful job even though we suspect it just might be leaching our soul away; might as well just turn our backs from the choices in the baskets completely and start sifting the sawdust through our fingers again—that's a whole lot easier.

One reason it's difficult to make choices is that, although all of us have limitations of one sort or another, it's actually rather shocking how much freedom we really have. If I wanted to, I could do something that addresses my yearning to do something more concretely practical to help other people. I could announce that I'm going to nursing school, for example. Or I could give in to my lifelong fascination with infant linguistic development, and get into graduate school. I could do it. And maybe I will.

We can approach the question of decision making from a number of perspectives, but if we're Christians, and if we really believe that we are made by God and live in a world made by

God and for God's purpose, our only reasonable starting place is that purpose: What does God want?

The Catholic spiritual tradition calls decision making "discernment." The word implies not coming up with a new idea completely out of our own creativity, but clarifying things so that we can see and understand something that's already in place: what God wants us to do.

St. Ignatius of Loyola, founder of the Society of Jesus, or the Jesuits, is really the king of discernment in the Catholic tradition. His *Spiritual Exercises,* written over a couple of decades in the mid-sixteenth century and used by hundreds of thousands in the centuries since, is essentially the structure of a personal retreat dedicated to discernment of God's will in one's life. This retreat could take as long as thirty days, and one of its last elements is this prayer:

> *Take Lord, and receive all my liberty, my memory, my understanding, and my entire will, all that I have and possess. Thou hast given all to me. To Thee, O Lord, I return it. All is Thine, dispose of it wholly according to Thy will. Give me Thy love and Thy grace, for this is sufficient for me.*[1]

It's called the Suscipe, Latin for "take," and even if you haven't prayed it before, it might be familiar to you from a contemporary hymn sung in Catholic churches called, not surprisingly, "Take Lord, Receive" and composed by, of course, a Jesuit.

If we're wondering what to do with our lives, or even with the next fifteen minutes, it's a wonderful prayer to fall back on. When it comes to decision making, context is everything, and this is a prayer that instantly puts our decision making into the right context, even when our own words fail us, when our own desires are pulling us in a million directions, and the sawdust is starting to look mighty appealing.

Although it doesn't use the word, the Suscipe is, in the end, about love. As Ignatius introduces the prayer in a section entitled "Contemplation to Attain the Love of God," he defines love. First he says that love is better expressed in actions than in words. Second, love is about what Ignatius calls a "mutual sharing of goods." Love, in other words, moves us to give to the one we love.[2]

After he describes love, Ignatius guides the retreatant to meditation. He should picture himself in the presence of God and the angels, giving thanks and praise to God. Ignatius's spiritual method is notable for its emphasis on imagination. We may think of this type of imaginative prayer as a new thing, or even outside the Christian tradition. It's not, and St. Ignatius is not the only Christian spiritual master to have encouraged the use of imagination in prayer.

Many of the meditations in the Exercises involve stories from the Gospels, for example, asking the retreatant to picture herself in the scene: as a "poor little unworthy slave" observing the Nativity, or speaking to Jesus as he hangs on the cross: "As I behold Christ in this plight, nailed to the cross, I shall ponder upon what presents itself to my mind."[3]

In this particular contemplation during the fourth and final week of the Exercises, the retreatant is called to ponder God's love. God loves you, and you know this because of all he has given you—from earthly life to eternal life. You love God, right? So how is that love expressed? What is the gift you give to God?

Take Lord, receive . . .

The more you roll this prayer around in your soul, and the more you think about it, the more radical it is revealed to be. All? A tall order. The tallest, even.

Remember that this prayer is to be used by a person who has been spending hours in meditation and prayer every day for thirty days. During this time, the person is engaged in a systematic reflection (honed by Ignatius over a twenty-year period) of his own sins and of the life of Christ, and the retreatant is considering the question of his own life in that intense context.

One of the primary themes presented to the retreatant is that of attachments and affections. Ignatius offers the account of "three classes of men" who have been given a sum of money, and who all want to rid themselves of it because they know their attachment to this worldly good impedes their salvation.

The first class would really like to rid themselves of the attachment, but the hour of death comes, and they haven't even tried. The second class would also like to give up the attachment, but do so, conveniently, without actually giving anything up.

Is this sounding familiar at all?

The third class wants to get rid of the *attachment* to the money, which they, like the others, know is a burden standing in the way. But they make no stipulations as to how this attachment is relinquished; they are indifferent about the method. Whatever God wants, they want. In a word, they are the free ones.

So, after thirty days or so, this is what the retreatant has worked up to. *Take Lord, receive* is possible only because the retreatant has opened himself to the reality of who God is, what God's purpose is for humanity, and what God has done for him in a particularly intense way.

The retreatant has seen that there is really no other response to life that does God justice. What love the Father has for us in letting us be called children of God, John says (1 John 3:1). What gift does our love prompt us to give?

In ages past, and probably in the minds of some of us still, that gift of self to God, putting oneself totally at God's disposal, is possible only for people called to a vowed religious life. Well, God didn't institute religious life in the second chapter of Genesis. He instituted marriage and family. I'm not a nun, but the Scriptures tell us repeatedly that all creation is groaning and being reborn and moving toward completion in God. Every speck of creation, everything that happens, every kid kicking a soccer ball down a road in Guatemala, each office worker in New Delhi, every ancient great-grandmother in a rest home in Boynton Beach, every baby swimming in utero at this moment around the world—all are beloved by God and are being constantly invited by him to love, and all can respond.

So yes, the Suscipe is a radical prayer of total self-giving. It's not a formula for easy decision making that we can adopt one morning after a lifetime of making decisions based on other, more prosaic or even selfish reasoning. It's the fruit of self-reflection and of openness to God's love.

But if it can get us out of the sawdust—why not?

veni creator spiritus

Come, Holy Ghost, Creator blest,
And in our souls take up your rest;
Come with your grace and heavenly aid
To fill the hearts which you have made.

O Comforter, to you we cry,
O heavenly gift of God Most High,
O fount of life and fire of love,
And sweet anointing from above.

You in your sevenfold gifts are known;
You, finger of God's hand we own;
You, promise of the Father, you
Who do the tongue with power imbue.

Kindle our senses from above,
And make our hearts overflow with love;
With patience firm and virtue high
The weakness of our flesh supply.

Far from us drive the foe we dread,
And grant us your peace instead;
So shall we not, with you for guide,
Turn from the path of life aside.

Oh, may your grace on us bestow
The Father and the Son to know;
And you, through endless times confessed,
Of both the eternal Spirit blest.

Now to the Father and the Son,
Who rose from death, be glory given,
With you, O holy Comforter,
Henceforth by all in earth and heaven.

Amen.

The Prayer of Power

They say that hindsight is 20/20, but is it always?

I can look back on my life and see what I could or should have done, but what I can't always recapture is how or why in the world I did what I did.

Exceptionally bad decisions puzzle me in hindsight, but so can the rare really good one, especially if there was difficulty in carrying it out. With lousy decisions I wonder, *What was I thinking?* With the good ones, I sometimes wonder how in the world I did it and where I got the strength.

And then I thank God, for I know that whatever it was, it didn't come from me alone.

It seems to me that thinking about the Holy Spirit is a little bit like this. We could, if we wanted to, drive ourselves slowly mad as we try to explain and analyze the triune God, and particularly the Holy Spirit, to ourselves and others.

There's a better way, though, a way that involves the same kind of hindsight we bring to the mystery of our own lives.

How did they do it? How could the church be born from this flawed, frightened bunch we call the apostles? The Gospels give us no hint, really, of what could possibly come after Jesus' earthly ministry, as the apostles stumble about, asking the wrong questions, giving the wrong answers, and running off just when it counted most.

Intellectual understanding does have its place, but it has its limits, also. Our relationship with God is like any other; it can be shipwrecked by not enough rational thinking or by too much.

So when we talk about out relationship to the Holy Spirit, we could unpack Trinitarian theology all day, and it would certainly help us see how God as Trinity is possible. But we might be better off letting our personal faith follow the paths that the early Christians trod. They didn't start with ideas or with a need to define God. They experienced God who did things and moved them to do things, and then they explained how in the world it all happened—it was because of the Holy Spirit, they said.

There are many prayers to the Holy Spirit, but one of the more commonly prayed and certainly the most beautiful is Veni Creator Spiritus, which is familiar to many of us in translation as the hymn "Come Holy Ghost." When you read it, or better yet pray it, you hear the echoes of the experience of early Christians. They discerned the truth and power of the Spirit, not through learning philosophy, but through understanding what the Spirit had wrought in their lives. They lived to tell the tale and, most important, to pass on the experience so it could be lived anew by us.

The prayer begins with a reference to the Spirit as Creator, pointing us to what Genesis tells us about God's Spirit hovering over the waters. The Spirit is Creator also in that God gave human beings life by sharing with them his breath—the Hebrew word for "breath" is also the word for "spirit."

Other Scriptural themes course through the prayer: Jesus' promise to send the Spirit as a Comforter. The apostles' experience at Pentecost—which indeed was a "fire of love" a "sweet anointing from above"—drove fear out, and gave the apostles power to speak.

This prayer alludes to the seven traditional gifts of the Holy Spirit, according to Isaiah 11:2–3: wisdom, understanding, counsel, fortitude, knowledge, piety, and fear of the Lord. You can also see hints of what Paul calls "the fruit of the Spirit" in Galatians 5:22–23: "love, joy, peace, patience, kindness, generosity, faithfulness, gentleness, self-control."

When we pray Veni Creator Spiritus, we're praying for all these same gifts and fruits, those that were so clearly and powerfully poured out in the early church. The apostles, justifiably frightened for their lives, locked themselves in a room in Jerusalem despite Jesus' words still alive in their memories: Go and baptize . . . I will send you an Advocate . . . Go out to all the world (Matthew 28:19; John 14:25–31).

Their tongues were tied, they were paralyzed by fear, they were at a loss for how to proceed until the Spirit empowered them with courage and wisdom, and they could pour out into the crowded city and share the Good News.

The Spirit came into their lives, and the church was born. They lived and moved and breathed in the Spirit, and then reflected on that experience. Paul's letters are testimonies to the reality and the power of the Spirit. We praise the Holy Spirit and pray that we might be open to that Spirit because we know that discipleship is impossible if we just depend on our own power. To love as Jesus did, we need the power of God strengthening us, and that power is the Holy Spirit.

Veni Creator Spiritus dates from the ninth century. It's attributed to all kinds of people from St. Ambrose to Charlemagne, but most scholars are reasonably certain that, if anyone deserves credit for this prayer, it's a fellow named Rabanus Maurus.

Rabanus Maurus was one of the most renowned scholars of early medieval Europe. He was, as is the case with so many of our renowned medieval scholars such as St. Albert the Great or St. Hildegarde of Bingen, an expert in almost every subject you can imagine.

Living and working during the reign of Charlemagne, Marcus was a ruler who sought to revitalize learning in a Christian context. He was actually taught by the Emperor's primary scholarly advisor, Alcuin. Following in his teacher's prolific mode, Maurus wrote commentaries on almost every book in the Bible, a twenty-two–book encyclopedia called *De universo,* and works on logic and grammar.

Sixty-four of his homilies have survived, homilies that provide an antidote to our stereotypes of ancient churchmen as nothing but purveyors of dry doctrine and stringent moral precepts. In one, for example, Maurus comments on some recent hysteria about an eclipse of the moon, recounting how townspeople are going outside at night raising all kinds of ruckus because they've been convinced that noise and spells are necessary to help God hold up the moon.

Patiently, Maurus works through the illogic of this and then carefully explains what an eclipse actually is. He invites his listeners to take this as just one more opportunity to praise God for the wonders of his creation. So much for religion's hostility to science. So much for the image of ancient Christianity as little more than superstition.[1]

Besides all this, Maurus wrote poems and hymns, including, many scholars believe, Veni Creator Spiritus. It's an apt prayer to come from this busy man, who not only wrote all the works mentioned above, but was also an abbot, an archbishop, and a dedicated servant of the poor who saw to it that during a famine, every day, three hundred people were fed out of his own home. We may wonder how he did it. Even through the mists of time, taking into account a little of that exaggeration with which we describe our saints, it seems fairly clear that Rabanus Maurus embodies the power of the Holy Spirit, the same Spirit that emboldened the apostles, the same Spirit that seeks a home in our own lives.

Veni Creator Spiritus has landed in various liturgical spots through history. In some liturgies, it was part of prayers said before Mass, either while a priest was vesting or even as he approached the altar. In some medieval liturgies, it was prayed during the offertory, after the gifts were laid on the altar, or during the priest's washing of his hands.[2]

It is prayed during the Liturgy of the Hours, the cycle of prayers that all priests and religious are asked to pray throughout the day and night. The basis of the Hours, or the Divine Office, is the Psalms, but it also includes many other prayers and readings from Scripture, as well as from spiritual writers of the past.

Veni Creator Spiritus, not surprisingly, has always been an important part of the Liturgy of the Hours during the Pentecost season, both during Vespers (Evening Prayer) and terce. Terce is the prayer time that occurs in mid-morning, usually around nine, and Veni Creator Spiritus found a place there because the Acts of the Apostles indicates that the Holy Spirit descended on the apostles around that time. As Peter defends the apostles to the crowds, he points out: "These people are not drunk, as you suppose, for it is only nine o'clock in the morning" (Acts 2:15).

It's also prayed and sung at papal elections, bishops' consecrations, confirmations, church councils and synods, and even at coronations of British monarchs.

Although Veni Creator Spiritus finds its place mostly in liturgical prayer, you will also find it in many Catholic prayer books, sometimes along with another famous prayer to the Holy Spirit, Veni Sancte Spiritus. The latter was probably written by Stephen Langton, a thirteenth-century Archbishop of Canterbury, and it is used as a "sequence"—a prayer that is recited or sung before the gospel on Pentecost Sunday.

Will I be participating in any papal elections in the near future? Probably not. But I think there is still room for Veni

Creator Spiritus in my prayer life. The world around me is filled with programs encouraging me to get motivated. I could pay lots of money learning how to find a spark and keep it burning. Or I could open myself to the Holy Spirit in any way I can, perhaps even through this prayer, which expresses the experience and wisdom of others, from the prophets of the Old Testament, to the apostles, to a very busy ninth-century Christian—an experience that told them where real power and motivation could be found.

When we look back on those rare good decisions, those moments when we did the right thing despite our myriad fears, we may wonder how we got through it, but if we're honest, we know. We really do. The reason the moment is mysterious is because we know the resources didn't come just from us. There was something else, and a lot of us would give that something else a name. The apostles knew it, Rabanus Maurus knew it, and so do we, because we've been touched by it: the spirit of God.

grace at meals

Bless us O Lord, and these thy gifts, which we are about to receive from thy bounty, through Christ, Our Lord. Amen.

We give you thanks, almighty God, for all your benefits, who live and reign, for ever and ever.

May the souls of the faithful departed, through the mercy of God, rest in peace. Amen.

The Prayer of Gratitude

Every family has a story about grace. Not the kind of grace from on high, but the kind that we mumble, stumble through, and declaim at the dinner table. I have a few.

My oldest son, called upon to say grace when he was a toddler, invented his own, "Dear God, thank you for this food. We love you very much. Amen."

Short and to the point. You can tell a hungry boy invented it. His younger brother picked it up, and even as teenagers, my terribly imaginative sons, if coerced into leading table prayer, would fall back on the words Christopher pulled together when he was three.

Katie was next, and she listened to her evangelical preschool teachers very carefully, so when it was her turn to start praying, it was in devoted imitation of them.

"Lord, Jesus," she would drawl in a low, serious voice, "Sank you for the good milk, the good bread," and here her eyes would rove around the table to see what was waiting, "the good chicken and eversing else. Help us be good and all take our naps." And then she'd shout, "A-nen!" and clap, having very nicely integrated into her young spiritual life the concept of religion as social control.

Now it's Joseph's turn, and he's two and a half, and he's not going to evangelical preschool. He walks around shrines with his breviary-praying dad, so his prayer is very Catholic. He slaps his chest a few times and says, "Son, Holy Spiwit, sank you" while shoveling mashed potatoes into his mouth with a butter knife.

You've noticed, perhaps, an absence of traditional prayers from this litany. Well, that's probably because while I was certainly raised Catholic, table prayer just wasn't part of our family life unless it was a holiday, and in those cases, my father prayed. This is probably why, when it's my turn, what still pops out of my mouth is the grace that you'll find more frequently on the lips of Protestants than Catholics: "Lord, we thank you for this food, and we ask you to bless it for the nourishment of our minds and our bodies in your service."

I don't believe that I ever heard that most common "official" formal Catholic grace that we'll be discussing in this chapter until I was a teenager. I was at a friend's house where they not only prayed before, but also *after* the meal. It struck me as a bit excessive, but that didn't stop me from also feeling a mite embarrassed because I didn't know the words, and I wondered if I should.

There are countless ways to thank God for our food, and by extension, our lives. And what's interesting is that gratitude is such a universal, deep-seated response, whether the words are spontaneous or ritualized.

"Grace" is derived from the Latin word *gratia,* which means thanksgiving. There is just something about sitting down with a meal in front of you—a meal that nourishes your body and your spirit—that prompts gratitude. It's a moment that focuses us. We may do lots of other things during our day, we may have big plans and tedious responsibilities, we may face tragedy and mystery, but we would be able to do none of it, we know, unless we were simply alive. For this we are truly grateful.

Prayer before and after meals is a fundamental element of Jewish life. The Torah reveals that the whole earth belongs to God. So before a meal, God is blessed. These prayers are called benedictions; they are prayers of praise and, as one writer puts it, "a way of asking for and receiving God's permission to take and enjoy that which belongs to Him."[1]

After the meal, thanksgiving is offered, an act that is explicitly called for in Deuteronomy: "But when you have eaten your fill, you must bless the LORD, your God, for the good country he has given you" (Deuteronomy 8:10).

While many people associate prayer with the time before we start eating, in Jewish tradition the prayer after the meal is a serious obligation as well. This not just because it is mandated by the Torah but also, some sages suggest, because it discourages our tendency to rush off and forget God once our needs have been satisfied.

Early Jewish Christians maintained the tradition of mealtime prayer. Paul alludes to the practice several times through his letters. In chapter 6 of his Gospel, John focuses on Jesus as the "bread of life" and describes Jesus giving thanks before he distributes the miraculously multiplied loaves and fish. And Jesus' blessing at the Last Supper is rooted in Jewish benedictions. You might think of the Eucharistic prayer as the grace we pray at God's banquet for his family.

Praying at meals is mentioned frequently in the writings of the church fathers. In the second century, the Christian theologian

Tertullian wrote, "But, withal, it becomes believers not to take food, and not to go to the bath, before interposing a prayer; for the refreshments and nourishments of the spirit are to be held prior to those of the flesh, and things heavenly prior to things earthly."[2]

A fourth-century document, attributed to St. Athanasius but probably not written by him, contains both before- and after-meal prayers recommended to Christians. The prayer before the meal alludes to the disparate grains that were gathered to make the bread and prays that the church, too, may be united in the kingdom. After the meal, thanksgiving is offered for both physical and spiritual nourishment in the hopes that those who've just eaten will be strengthened in both body and soul.

There are plenty of examples of table prayers from medieval times, because they were used both in the secular world and in monastic life. Schoolchildren were taught graces for mealtime, the aristocracy employed clergy whose responsibilities included leading prayer before meals, and monastic rules described sometimes intricate and involved graces, some early examples of which dictated that each dish should be blessed separately before it was presented to the community.

For modern Catholics, the most commonly known and recited grace is the traditional "Bless us, O Lord, for these thy gifts . . ." prayed before the meal. For some (like my friend's family), a prayer of thanksgiving is recited afterward, which begins "We give you thanks, O Lord," and sometimes ends with a prayer for the faithful departed.

You can hear the echo of Jewish ancestry in this prayer, a prayer of blessing before the meal and a prayer of thanksgiving afterward. This grace that so many of us know and say is actually just a small part of a longer prayer, the more or less "official" prayer at meals that was part of the traditional Roman Breviary.

We've alluded to the breviary, or Liturgy of the Hours, or Divine Office, many times. It's the ancient cycle of prayers that have their roots in the regular Jewish recitation of the Psalms. From very early in the church's history, Christians imitated this practice and developed it further. All priests and religious are supposed to pray some form of the Liturgy of the Hours every day. The prayers begin in the morning and stretch into the night, and for centuries included prayers for meals.

These traditional prayers before and after meals that so many of us learned were really condensed versions of what priests and religious were doing in community. There were two sets: one for the midday meal and another for the evening meal. The prayers were composed with a communal setting in mind, so they have a liturgical quality to them, with parts and responses, a silent, individual recitation of the Lord's Prayer, and ample reliance on the Psalms. What you'll find at the end of both before-meal prayers is, "Bless us, O Lord." And at the end of both after-meal prayers is, "We give you thanks, O Lord . . ." along with the prayer for the dead. The "Bless us, O Lord" prayer, which eventually found its way into popular usage, is actually pretty old, appearing in an eighth-century book of prayers.[3]

So back and forth it goes. As Christians, we continue blessing God and thanking him as our Jewish ancestors did. We connect this earthly food to the spiritual nourishment that God promises now and forever; we see that when we gather for a meal in community, we're experiencing a taste of heaven. The monks and religious ritualize it, pulling in the ancient Psalms, the prayer for our daily bread taught to us by Jesus, and a hope that all might one day share in that heavenly banquet. And the rest of us join, at least in part, in the most important part of blessing and thanking. And God's people, from youngest to oldest, wherever they dwell, are one in thanking God for this meal, and for life.

Gratitude, someone once said, is the heart of prayer. And I think that person was right. Gratitude for a meal is really just an extension of the gratitude we're called to live in all day long.

There are times when my life is not what I want or think it should be. It might be a small aggravation or a huge worry, but the bottom line is, I don't like it and I'm not happy with it. A while back, I decided that anger, frustration, and wishful thinking got me nowhere. Forget what could be, I decided, and concentrate on what is and where God is in all of it. Instead of thinking "I wish" or "If only" or something more profane, I started forcing myself to simply think (or pray), "Thank you."

You'd be amazed at what that does to change your perspective instantly.

My youngest son, for a time, when he was just learning to talk, got some of his words mixed up. Specifically, he thought that "thank you" and "okay" were the same. So for a couple of months, Joseph, delighted in his growing verbal skills, said, "Thank you!" (or at that point, "ank you") to everything.

"Joseph, eat your peas." "Ank you!"

"Joseph, go to the car." "Ank you!"

"Joseph, it's time for bed." "Ank you!"

He was, we concluded, either very confused or the most grateful human being on the planet.

None of us can say everything we feel all the time. The words we utter and the gestures we make put into time and space, express the fundamental stance that supports and moves us. When I say, "I love you," I don't mean that I love only for that moment. So when I pause before a meal to give blessing and thanks, I'm doing the same. I'm always grateful (I hope), and here, before the meal that is, in a way, a symbol for all God is and does for me, I respond with words that symbolize (I hope) the response I'm living in my life.

G. K. Chesterton, the famed Catholic convert and writer, once said:

> You say grace before meals. All right. But I say grace before the concert and the opera, and grace before the play and pantomime, and grace before I open a book, and grace before sketching, painting, swimming, fencing, boxing, walking, playing, dancing, and grace before I dip the pen in the ink.[4]

For this, all of this, we are truly grateful.

the liturgy of the hours

Blessed be the Lord,
The God of Israel;
He has come to His people and set them free.
He has raised up for us a mighty Saviour,
Born of the house of His servant David.
Through His holy prophets He promised of old
That He would save us from our enemies,
From the hands of all who hate us.
He promised to show mercy to our fathers
And to remember His holy Covenant.
This was the oath He swore to our father Abraham:
To set us free from the hands of our enemies,
Free to worship Him without fear,
Holy and righteous in His sight

All the days of our life.
You, My child shall be called
The prophet of the Most High,
For you will go before the Lord to prepare His way,
To give his people knowledge of salvation
By the forgiveness of their sins.
In the tender compassion of our Lord
The dawn from on high shall break upon us,
to shine on those who dwell in darkness
And the shadow of death,
And to guide our feet into the way of peace.
Glory to the Father,
and to the Son,
and to the Holy Spirit.
As it was in the beginning.
is now, and will be forever.
Amen.

The Prayer of the Church

The traditional vocal prayers in this book have come from many places and from every impulse and yearning of the human soul. They've been shaped by culture, politics, and the wear and tear of being used, tested, enriched, and honed.

One theme that keeps emerging, one common thread that keeps insistently being woven through so many of our accounts, though, is this thing called the Liturgy of the Hours.

We've also referred to it as breviary prayers, the Divine Office, or just the Office or the Hours. So many of our prayers have been shaped in the context of the Hours, or have emerged to echo the purpose and hope of the Hours in the lives of ordinary people, that it's worth taking a look at what the Liturgy of the Hours is.

Very simply put, the Liturgy of the Hours is a daily cycle of prayers scheduled to be prayed at specific points of the day in the name of the entire church. They begin with Morning Prayer, which always and everywhere, for example, includes the *Canticle of Zechariah* or *Benedictus* quoted at the beginning of this chapter and taken from Luke 1:68–79. The purpose is to sanctify the day, to offer praise to God, and in some sense, to live in the spirit of Paul's call to "pray without ceasing" (1 Thessalonians 5:17).

There are two common images associated with the Hours: monks or nuns chanting in a chapel, and priests looking up from a small bound volume, nodding at an interruption, "Well, I'm just praying my Office, but it can wait for a moment."

What's going on in both of these scenes is the praying of the Liturgy of the Hours, an essential, foundational set of prayers of the church. They are prayed around the clock throughout the year by clergy, religious, and the laity, and the form they take today is quite close to the form they've had from at least the fourth century.

In a country and society such as ours, in which there are plenty of Catholics but not any sort of widespread, permeating Catholic culture, and certainly not a thriving monastery or convent in every town, we are not nearly as aware of the praying of the Hours as European Christians were from the Middle Ages through much of the nineteenth century, when almost every major church, especially cathedrals, held not only daily Mass but also at least Lauds (morning prayer) and Vespers (evening prayer). In this context, there was a strong sense that this daily liturgical prayer was a vital prayer of the entire church. This daily cycle of prayers, along with the Mass, was the context in which all our individual prayers were developed.

But the prayer is still going on, whether or not you and I see it. Every priest that you know is supposed to pray the Hours. Every religious community still prays the Hours, somehow and in some fashion. In a growing number of parishes, you'll find parts of the Hours being prayed: perhaps Morning Prayer offered before daily Mass, or Vespers offered in the evening.

And you may even know lay Catholics who pray some form of the Office themselves throughout the day.

The Hours have evolved and have been reformed many times over the centuries, but at present they begin with Lauds in the morning, followed by terce (midmorning), sext (noon), and none (midafternoon), then Vespers in the evening, and Compline, which is also called Night Prayer. There's also the Office of Readings, which can be prayed any time during the day, but which religious communities that are committed to emulating more ancient forms place in the middle of the night at two or three in the morning, during what used to be called Matins. During one of my visits to a monastery, I vowed to make it to Matins. Needless to say, when the moment came, I changed my mind and let the bell ring on.

The bare minimum of the cycle that you must pray in order to be considered as keeping the Divine Office includes Lauds, Vespers, and one of the midday prayers of your choice. Religious communities that pray the Hours "in choir," or in common, are supposed to pray all these midday hours. The ideal for praying the Hours is to do so with others; it's a liturgy, after all. Most individuals and communities pray the Hours in the vernacular language, but very few still use Latin.

The text of the Hours, centered around the Psalms first, then other Scripture readings, and selections from other spiritual writers and preachers, is promulgated from the Vatican and found in a book—several, actually. The book for the Hours most commonly used to be called a breviary, but it's not supposed to be called that anymore. The full Liturgy of the Hours fills up four volumes (one for Advent and Christmas, one for Lent and Easter, and two for Ordinary Time), although there are plenty of abbreviated, single-volume versions available that adapt the Hours for various settings and uses.

The impulse behind the Hours is an ancient one, as ancient as the Psalms, some composed as early as the tenth century, that form its core: "Seven times a day I praise you" (Psalm 119:164). Structured, thrice-daily prayer at morning, afternoon, and evening, was incorporated into Jewish life in Palestine by the fifth century before Christ. Early Jewish Christians continued participating in these communal prayers as we can see, for example, from the story of Peter, John, and a crippled beggar in Acts 3. Peter and John meet the beggar on their way "to the temple area for the three o'clock hour of prayer."

Near the end of the first century, Christian practice was completely distinct from Judaism. Praying the Psalms, however, remained an integral part of Christian worship, both during Mass and during the communal prayer that many Christians gathered for in the mornings, evenings, and especially on the Vigils before Sunday and important feasts.

Praying the Hours of the day with the Psalms took a more concrete form in the second through fifth centuries, as Christian monasticism emerged in the deserts of North Africa and the Middle East, and then spread to Europe. During this era, when spiritual and ascetic enthusiasm could run very high and was in some cases almost an extreme sport, some enthusiasts prayed their way through the entire Psalter—all 150 Psalms—every single day.

St. Benedict, who is considered the father of Western monasticism, gave his monks of the sixth century one of the earliest surviving schedules of praying the Hours, dividing the day into the eight hours starting with the middle-of-the-night offices, throughout the day until Compline. His Rule details, for example, that on ordinary days (not Sundays or feasts), Lauds begins with Psalm 66, which is to be chanted slowly, so that everyone can get there on time for the beginning of the next part, which is Psalm 50. This is followed by two more Psalms, praises, a selection from a Pauline epistle, responses, a hymn, another canticle (from the Gospels, such as the Magnificat), and then a litany.

Over the next millennium, the Hours developed in two different parts of Christian life. First was the monastic form, which was longer, embraced all the traditional Hours of the day, and usually incorporated all the Psalms into the prayer over the course of a week (except for the fellows who were trying to do it all in a day).

But in the growing cities and towns, the practice of the Hours was taking another, simpler shape. The emphasis was on Lauds and Vespers, there were fewer Psalms used, and they tended to include more non-biblical material including, as the Middle Ages wore on, stories (increasingly fantastic and legendary in nature) of saints and their deeds.

In the sixteenth century, after the Protestant Reformation, the Roman Catholic Church engaged in an extended, cleansing self-reformation of its own. The Council of Trent met in several sessions over the years to reaffirm Catholic doctrine and to clean up Catholic practice, including that of the Liturgy of the Hours.

The result, in 1568, was called the Breviary, and it was a serious attempt to streamline the Hours and ensure that the liturgy echoed the beauty and simplicity of the psalmist's prayers. It was to be used by all who prayed what was then called the Divine Office, except for religious orders and local rites more than 200 years old that had their own forms of the Hours.

A few hundred years later, the Second Vatican Council called for another major revision of the Liturgy of the Hours, as it did for all the church's liturgy, from top to bottom. The revision was completed in 1971.

The result is the form I described at the beginning of the chapter. The prayers were first tied to the hours of the day. During the preceding centuries, as the recitation of the Office took on the weight of obligation, as spiritual practices often unfortunately do, not a few began trying to make things easier on themselves by collapsing prayer sessions into one another or getting through their prayer obligations in a single session. French king Louis XIII's prime minister, Cardinal Richelieu, worked out a system in which he prayed the Office every other day. He'd get all of Monday done between eleven and midnight on Monday, and then take care of Tuesday from midnight to one in the morning, freeing him until Wednesday night. Since the point of the Hours, historically, had been to sanctify every hour of the day, this system obviously missed the point.

Lauds and Vespers were put at the center in the 1971 revision as the most necessary elements of the Hours. Options for use of the midday prayers were introduced. Matins, that middle-of-the-night prayer, was dropped and replaced with the similarly structured Office of Readings that could be prayed any time. The whole Psalter was spread out over a four-week period, rather than one week, as had previously been the case.

But the most important thing that this revision tried to accomplish was to reintroduce the Liturgy of the Hours as the prayer of the whole church, not just of the clergy and religious. In the documents that accompany the revision, which you can find in the beginning of any edition of the Hours, the Hours are constantly spoken of as the prayer of the church, as one offered by the entire church. This prayer may be prayed mostly by priests and religious, but they are not doing so in their own name, simply for their own benefit; they are praying on behalf of all of us.[1]

But that doesn't mean that any or all of us can't pray the Hours. We're encouraged to do so, and we're encouraged to see our own prayer, no matter what the form, in the context of the Liturgy of the Hours.

This is actually what happened many times during the church's history. As we've seen, the rosary grew out of the people's desire to emulate in some way the praying of the Divine Office. They may not have been able to pray all the Psalms, but they could pray 150 Pater Nosters or Ave Marias.

The Hail Mary in its present form grew out of the *Little Office of the Virgin Mary,* another, shorter version of the Hours, which may have started in religious communities but quickly became very popular in the outside world.

Through the centuries, there also have been a number of shortened books of the Hours and breviaries used by lay people.

Beginning in the 1920s and led by renewed European scholarship and (mostly) Benedictine efforts, a real liturgical revival began in the church, one that may have climaxed in the work of the Second Vatican Council but certainly bore fruit before then. One of the fruits was a revived interest in the praying of the Hours, and one of the most powerful tools for this in the United States was something called *A Short Breviary*.

The first edition of *A Short Breviary* was published in 1941. It's a greatly simplified and clearly organized single volume of daily prayer of the Hours as prayed by the Benedictines and published by their St. John's Abbey Press in Collegeville, Minnesota. The edition I have came out in 1944 and has two forewords. In the first, dated 1942, the abbot of St. John's expresses anticipation of the upcoming fourteenth centenary of St. Benedict's life and great delight that "the enthusiastic reception accorded the first edition of this breviary is evidence that the laity are ready to take intelligent possession of their rightful heritage."[2]

The second foreword is somber, indicating that times have changed. As it turned out, the centenary was not celebrated because of the ravages of war and more particularly because St. Benedict's original abbey in Monte Cassino, Italy, had been destroyed.

But this terrible world war, if we may draw an inference from the demand for *A Short Breviary,* has apparently served to bring home to many souls the need of living in the spirit of St. Benedict. May the third printing of *A Short Breviary* help to increase the number of those who delight in singing the praise of God according to the mind of His Church.[3]

One American Catholic who appreciated *A Short Breviary* was the great fiction writer, Flannery O'Connor. Suffering from lupus, living in rural southern Georgia, and writing her books filled with misfits and prophets, O'Connor read the *Summa Theologica* for fifteen minutes every night before bed and prayed with the *Short Breviary.* In 1956, she sent a copy to a friend who had just become Catholic, saying:

> Anyway, don't think I am suggesting that you read the office every day. It's just a good thing to know about, I say Prime in the morning and sometimes I say Compline at night but usually I don't. But anyway I like parts of my prayers to stay the same and part to change. So many prayer books are so awful, but if you stick with the liturgy, you are safe.[4]

There are scores of ways to pray and scads of guides to help you do it. Most are worth something, some are awful, some may seem perfect. But when in doubt, stick with the liturgy. When feeling as St. Paul did, that you do not know how to pray as you ought and when your own personal prayers just seem awful, stick with the liturgy.

Centuries of yearning for the divine, millennia of questions, anger, and praise are brought together in the structure of the Hours, ready for us to just plug our own lives into it. Kathleen Norris, a poet and spiritual writer, spent months living in the same St. John's Abbey that produced *A Short Breviary,* but decades later. The fruit of her time there is the rich and beautiful *The Cloister Walk.* In it, she writes of the praying of the Psalms with the Benedictines:

> You come to the Bible's great "book of praises" through all the moods and conditions of life, and while you may feel like hell, you sing anyway. To your surprise, you find that the psalms do not deny your true feelings but allow you to reflect on them, right in front of God and everyone. . . . The liturgy that Benedictines have been experimenting with for fifteen-hundred-plus years taught me the value of tradition; I came to see that the psalms are holy in part because they are so well used. If so many generations had found solace here, might I also?[5]

There's something else, too, about the Hours. Sometimes my prayer seems so small. Doesn't yours? So terribly self-referential, more of a hapless exercise in self-examination, with a horizon only as far as the wall of my room. I forget that there is something else going on, that there is a world groaning as it labors toward God, that the whole world is God's, that all creation sings his praise, that what I think, say, and do is a part of this. I suspect my prayer is or can be bigger than I think. But how? "The divine Office is the voice of the Church, that is the whole mystical body publicly praising God."[6]

What a change, what a seismic shift in my spiritual life as I consider this. It is not, after all, merely about me. It is about God and what God is doing in the world—what God is doing in the world through the Body of Christ.

So surely not eight times a day, and perhaps not even more than once, but go ahead, I say as I crack open that book, ribbons marking ancient words of praise. *Plug me in; I'm Catholic,* I feel like saying as I listen to past and present echoes and see shadows emerge from darkness, eyeing me with patient amusement as I find my place. I sense those other pilgrims who have been nourished at this same spring to go out, dwell with the poor, soothe the suffering, and embrace the dying. Yes, I'm Catholic. But now—I want to join the church.

Lord, open my lips;
my mouth will proclaim your praise.
(Psalm 51:17)

glory
be

Glory to the Father, and to the Son, and to the Holy Spirit:
as it was in the beginning, is now, and will be forever.
Amen.

Words of Praise

Sometimes—not often, but once every few months or so—you have vast expanses of time for prayer, to meditate for a bit, read some Scripture, contemplate and listen.

But other times, you just need a prayer in a pinch. Catholics have that.

Take the Glory Be. If you were raised Catholic or spent a lot of time around praying Catholics, you've probably heard it once or twice. Someone's about to go on a trip, start a meeting or, for some other reason, just feels that everyone needs to pray right this minute.

We could make something up, and sometimes we do. But other times we don't. We feel awkward, we can't think, or we want everyone to pray together. So we turn to a faithful, dependable trio: "Let's say an Our Father, Hail Mary, and a Glory Be, okay?"

If this strikes you as odd, think again, and count your blessings. It could be worse (or better, depending on your point of view). I have a friend with Very Serious Catholic relations. She swears that if there's a lull in the conversation, the Very Serious Catholic sister-in-law will slap her hands on her knees and declare, "Let's all say a rosary." No wonder my friend's daughters talk so much. They learned their lesson early.

It's a short prayer—we don't even say it at Mass—but the Glory Be is still one of the basics of our repertoire. It sums up everything our prayer has been (or should have been) about, points us in the right direction and attaches us to the divine and the eternal. It's like a final "I love you" at the end of a phone conversation. It's our "praise the Lord" and our "thank you Jesus."

Now, if you were like I was as a child, you might have wondered why Catholics have two such similar prayers. We've got the sign of the cross; why bother with the Glory Be? They're basically the same, aren't they?

What a difference a couple of words makes. Yes, they both ground us in the truth about God: Father, Son, and Holy Spirit. But the sign of the cross, in which we pray "in the name of . . ." is, among other things, a declaration of identity. In it, we take our stand and declare to whom we're praying and whom we trust to respond to those prayers.

But the Glory Be is different. It's much more cosmic, really. The sign of the cross is like a wedding ring. The Glory Be is like an "I love you" whispered before surgery.

The Glory Be evolved as a closing prayer of sorts for all kinds of situations. It closes each decade of the rosary. In the Divine Office, which is the prayer that all religious are supposed to say throughout the day, a form of the Glory Be ends many of the Psalms.

The Glory Be is actually a specific kind of prayer. It's called a doxology, or "words of praise" (from *doxa*–"glory" and *logos*–"word"). The Glory Be is often called the "lesser doxology" in contrast to the "greater doxology"–the Gloria we sing at Mass, which begins with the angels' praise of God from Luke's story of the Nativity (Luke 2:14).

Doxologies were a common part of Jewish prayer. In fact, if you flip through the book of Psalms, you'll find five of them, one at the end of each section of Psalms. For example, Psalms 1–41 are considered a single section, and Psalm 41 ends with "Blessed be the LORD, the God of Israel, from all eternity and forever. Amen. Amen" (Psalms 41:14). You'll find similar words at the end of Psalms 72, 89, 106 and then, ending the entire collection, in Psalm 150, a total hymn of praise, to punctuate the book of Psalms.

The book of Psalms is not exactly free from strife, pain, and questions. The psalmist writes out of joy, but just as often out of fear, anger, and desolation (try reading Psalm 137 to get a taste of that bitter drink). But punctuating each section, and then, the entire book, are these doxologies. It's as if the psalmist is saying, All of this mess happens, and life is woven of gorgeous and tattered thread. But God is great, and God endures, and blessed be God.

That tradition carried through to early Christian discourse and prayer. There are doxologies in Paul's letters (Ephesians 3:21 is a good example) as well as in the book of Revelation (7:12).

The *Didache* is that (probably) second-century manual of Christian practice that gives us insight into the early adaptation of Matthew's version of the Lord's Prayer, and it's useful when we're exploring the issue of doxologies, as well. For in the *Didache*'s explanation of what we'd call the eucharistic prayer, we find several moments of praise: "For Thine is the glory and the power through Jesus Christ for ever." "To Thee be the glory for ever."

At around the time the *Didache* was composed, Christian doxologies began to reflect the growing understanding of God's triune nature. Polycarp was a bishop of Smyrna who was arrested during a persecution and taken to the arena to be tried. It's hard not to be impressed by Polycarp's pointed yet subtle defiance as he's instructed to say "away with the atheists" (meaning the Christians, who didn't believe in Roman gods, and thus were atheists from the Roman viewpoint). The account tells us that Polycarp complies by looking earnestly at the gathered crowd of pagans and then looking up to heaven and "groaning, 'Away with the atheists!'"

The account of St. Polycarp's martyrdom isn't notable only because it's one of the earliest, most complete accounts of Christian martyrdom. It's also one of the first sources in which we find an explicitly Trinitarian doxology, uttered by Polycarp as he was tied to a stake in the middle of a pyre.

"I praise thee, I bless thee, I glorify thee, through our eternal High Priest in heaven, thy beloved Son Jesus Christ, by whom and with whom be glory to thee and the Holy Ghost, now and for all ages to come. Amen."[1]

And then they lighted the fire and Polycarp's martyrdom began.[2]

Throughout the early church, we find these kinds of doxologies in various forms in the liturgy and especially attached to the Psalms, which were recited throughout the day, just as they were in Judaism, and just as they are by religious men and women today. In 529, a church council standardized the form, which was, in Latin: *Gloria Patri, et Filio, et Spiritu Sancto, sicut erat in principio et semper, et in saecula saeculorum. Amen.*

Just as with the sign of the cross and the creed, the Glory Be reflects the theological concerns of the early church. Those early Christian doxologies that we find in Paul and the *Didache* aren't strongly Trinitarian in nature. After Polycarp, that Trinitarian formulation pops up consistently a couple of hundred years later, as the divinity of Jesus and the Holy Spirit are challenged, then thought through, and more explicitly articulated. Thus evolved a fuller understanding of what Jesus himself said in Matthew 28: "Go, therefore, and make disciples of all nations, baptizing them in the name of the Father, and of the Son, and of the holy Spirit" (Matthew 28:19).

The Glory Be was attached to the rosary here and there in various spots in Europe in the sixteenth century, and has remained there ever since in popular devotion. Most of the time, official descriptions of the rosary—in church documents listing approved prayers or in papal encyclicals—don't mention the Glory Be. But we say it anyway, because over decades and centuries, those who prayed it knew intuitively that it was fitting. It is yet one more example of how the interplay between authority and popular devotion in Catholicism is far more flexible than we might think.

The Glory Be is a way we close our prayer, the prayer in which we've laid our lives open before God. And then, after we have done all this, after we have thanked, questioned, and pondered, we offer praise:

> *Glory be to the Father, and to the Son, and to the Holy Spirit. As it was in the beginning, is now, and ever shall be, world without end, Amen.*

We've said our piece, laid out our needs, offered our gratitude, tried to listen, and now it's time to move along out into the rest of life as it will present itself to us in the next hour, the rest of the day, and through the night.

And no matter what it holds, we pray, "Glory be . . ."

amen

Amen.

We Say Yes

The *amen,* like the sign of the cross that began our book, is usually spoken so quickly and thoughtlessly that we think of it more as punctuation than prayer.

It may be true that you won't find a separate entry for *amen* in any Catholic prayer book. It's only one word, after all. But it really does deserve some attention on its own, for in its fullest, most traditional usage *amen* is much more than an ending tacked onto a prayer that we have uttered ourselves. In fact, that particular usage of saying "amen" at the end of one's own prayer is infrequent, largely prohibited in Judaism, for example, and works to eclipse the word's real power and deepest meaning. *Amen* is not an ending. It's a response. It doesn't mean "the end." It means "yes."

Amen is a Hebrew word that still plays an important and very particular role in Jewish prayer, so we'll start there to see how this role illuminates the way we have used it in the Christian context.

There is no simple translation of *amen* from Hebrew to English. It suggests establishing and affirming something with certainty and truth, and it appears throughout the Hebrew Scriptures on the lips of the assembled people as means of taking an oath and/or affirming a blessing—or a curse.

In Deuteronomy 27, for example, the people of Israel have reached the border of the Promised Land. Moses, who will see Canaan but not enter it, gives detailed instructions for what kind of people the Israelites are to be. Part of that instruction is a series of curses he tells the priests to announce when they enter—curses on those who dishonor their parents, who violate the rights of the poor, and so on. To each curse, the people are to answer, "Amen!"

In other parts of Scripture, the people answer "amen" to the priests' prayer of praise before the Ark of the Covenant (1 Chronicles 16:36), to a call to treat each other fairly upon their return from the Babylonian Exile (Nehemiah 5:13), and in the context of a psalm: "Blessed be the LORD, the God of Israel, from everlasting to everlasting! Let all the people say, Amen!" (Psalm 106:48).

Even today, Jewish tradition is quite specific about the use of "amen" in prayer. With a single, very specific exception—the third blessing after a meal—it is only to be used as Scripture suggests, as a response to a blessing or prayer offered by another, not as the end to one's own prayer.

In Jewish practice, the recitation of traditional prayers is the root of spiritual life. Sometimes one recites these prayers oneself, and at other times, one listens as they are offered by another person. Saying "amen" at the end of a blessing offered by another is an affirmation of everything that has been said, an added prayer that what has been prayed for will happen, and, in the end, a way of participating in the recitation of the blessing oneself, making it one's own.

In Hebrew, "amen" is made up of three letters, which, one sage taught, stood for the three words that mean "God, Faithful

King," so saying the word is also a way of acknowledging God's rule over the earth and one's life.[1]

Rabbis teach that "amen" should be pronounced carefully and distinctly, making sure that the vowel sound and the final *n* are heard. In Sephardic Hebrew, which is rooted in the Middle East, "amen" is offered after the blessing is completely finished, and in a tone no louder than the blessing itself.[2]

In the New Testament, *amen* is used in various contexts. Paul indicates that the congregational "amen" as a response to prayer remains a part of Christian worship (1 Corinthians 14:16), but he also adds an "amen" to the end of some of his doxologies (Romans 11:36).

In Revelation, Jesus is called "the Amen" (Revelation 3:14), meaning that he is God's affirmation of all that God has said and done. Jesus himself uses the word, and although the Gospels were written in Greek, "amen" is transliterated and appears in its Hebrew form. When Jesus uses it in the Gospels, some English versions don't translate it ("Amen, I say to you") and others do, rendering it as "truly" or, in older translations, "verily." In John's Gospel, uniquely, Jesus' usage of the word is consistently doubled, "Amen, amen, I say to you" (John 8:58, for example).

As that passage from Paul's letter to the Corinthians indicates, Christians seem to have carried over the traditional Jewish usage of *amen* as a response to their own separate worship. The clearest indication of the importance of *amen* to early Christian prayer is in a work by Justin Martyr, a second-century Christian philosopher who was, as his title indicates, martyred under Roman rule.

In his *First Apology,* written as an explanation of Christian belief and practice, Justin describes what we now call the Mass, and his description is striking because we might be surprised at how the essence and basic structure remain exactly the same from the past to the present.

In his narration of the Eucharistic prayer, Justin writes, "When he has finished the prayers and the thanksgiving, the whole congregation present assents, saying 'Amen.' 'Amen' in the Hebrew language means, 'so be it.'"[3]

As the liturgy developed over the centuries, the usage of *amen* developed along with it, but not in a straight line, although what we now call the "Great Amen" at the end of the Eucharistic prayer always maintained a place of primary importance. Some ancient prayer books indicate the use of *amen* as a congregational response to the presider's prayers; others also seem to imply that the presider himself is to add *amen* at the end of his own prayers.

From very early on, though, the one spot that you would find "amen" on the lips of Christians during liturgy besides the Great Amen was upon receiving communion. We see it very early, for example, in the catechetical instruction of St. Cyril of Jerusalem.

Although Cyril gave these twenty-four instructions to catechumens in the fourth century, they are well worth reading today for the clear light they shed on Christian faith and practice, even these sixteen centuries later. As he instructs them on receiving communion, he says:

> In approaching therefore, come not with thy wrists extended, or thy fingers spread; but make they left hand a throne for the fight, as for that which is to receive a King. And having hollowed thy palm, receive the Body of Christ, saying over it, Amen…Then after thou has partaken of the Body of Christ, draw near also to the Cup of His Blood; not stretching forth thine hands, but bending, and saying with an air of worship and reverence, Amen, hallow thyself by partaking also of the Blood of Christ.[4]

In some cases, recipients are described as not only saying "amen" but also kissing the hand of the one who gave them communion, especially when there was a bishop involved. We have at least one hint of this post-communion moment being used for political purposes. Novatian was a heretic who told his own followers that instead of saying "amen" after receiving communion they should say, "I will not go back to Pope Cornelius."

One day, while in the midst of writing this chapter, I went to Mass with my daughter, and because my husband had gone earlier, the toddler could stay at home with him. For the first time in almost three years, I could really attend to what was going on around and in front of me, relatively undistracted.

And because I was thinking about *amen,* I really noticed it. I noticed that when the priest prayed all those prayers he utters alone—the greeting, the various blessings, the opening prayer, and right up through the end, to the prayer after communion, and in the statement he makes to me about who I am receiving— I am asked to say *amen*. For the first time in a long time, it struck me that I was being invited to not merely say it, but to pray it, a stance that then pushes me back and challenges me to actually listen a little more carefully to what I'm assenting to, what I'm affirming, what I'm saying I believe is true, and, as a result, what I, too, am praying.

Amen is anything but a period on the end of a sentence. It's our prayer, our moment to affirm that we have joined our spirits to the prayers just spoken and that they are our prayers as well.

In a way, *amen* pushes us to attend to what is going on inside us when we pray. Vocal, composed prayer has a tendency to give us the jitters, because we're afraid that if we're not talking, we're not praying. We define participation by how much noise we make and how many words we say.

Amen alerts us to the fact that this is just not so. Jesus warns us against babbling on incessantly in prayer, and every mystic worth her salt tells us that what is important are not the words that come out of our mouths but the nature of the yearnings of our hearts. *Amen* can be another way of trying to learn that, as we affirm what we have prayed in silence. *Amen* is the fruit of joining our hearts to prayers spoken by others, prayers that have, in turn, emerged from the life of the Christians past and present.

Although *amen* is primarily a prayer of response, we're not saying that we shouldn't end our personal prayers with *amen,* too, as so many of us are in the habit of doing. There's no should or shouldn't about it. Ending our own prayers with "amen" is an affirmation that we've meant what we've said, that there's been no deception, and that it's all true.

But in the end, it all does indeed come back to response. This is why, as uncomfortable as it makes some who like their church services quiet and controlled, the Evangelical and Pentecostal tradition of offering *amen* in response to the preacher's words is actually quite biblical. Its roots are on the other side of the Jordan River, as God's people listened carefully to who God was calling them to be, and they answered, yes, this is who they would be.

"And all the people shall answer, 'Amen!'" Moses says, and the people still, in the same spirit, say "amen." They say it in the synagogue, at the table, at rising, and at retiring. They say it at Mass and during sermons. They say it as they murmur their own prayers and as they receive Jesus, God's own *Amen,* in the Eucharist.

Truly, verily, so be it. Yes.

Where Do My Prayers Go?

My prayer life, quite honestly, has improved dramatically over the past three years, and not because I've gotten terribly saintly.

An objective observer would look at what's happened during that time and think that the reason probably lies in the birth of my fourth child, my mother's death, a career change, and my father's cancer. And that observer might be correct.

But there's something else, not quite as obvious, that's at work here. Over the past three years, my two oldest sons have left home and gone to college.

And boy, have I prayed. I was desperate, so I prayed.

Worried about everything, I prayed. Concerned that they weren't adjusting, I prayed. Annoyed that they seemed to be adjusting way too well, I prayed. They don't eat or sleep enough, so they can't shake their colds; they get swamped at the end of the semesters; they doubt themselves; they run up against hard, sad situations; and they're hours away.

So, trying to let go and let God take care of them now, because that's what's supposed to happen, I pray.

I don't presume to know exactly how it works as the prayers leave my mouth or beat along with my heart, but this is what happens quite often these days: My youngest son, who is two years old, needs me many times a day. A typical two-year-old, he bumps his head or hurts his finger or just wants to sit on my lap. I hold him close, knowing as I do how quickly these days pass, and I wrap my heart around him. *God bless him. God protect him, let him know your love.* And then, because I can't hold back, and because I know that somehow there is a part of me that dwells with God where there is no time or space, and that my boys live there too, I hold my other two sons, my big boys, far away, and I try to wrap them in the prayer, too. And Katie, too. *All of these children, Lord. Open their hearts, comfort them, and guide them. God, just beat some sense into them.*

And then the mothers get to hear me: Mary and St. Monica, because they know.

I don't know exactly what these prayers are all about, but I do know that I have to do it, and they come out of the truest place inside me. I confess that I pray a lot more these days because I love my grown sons, I see them three or four times a year, and I have to do something besides nag, listen, and send cookies. So, up against the walls of earthly limits, I pray my way past them to love my kids.

Our prayers are as different and as variously motivated as we are. But even the most confident among us might sometimes wonder: Why am I doing this? Why am I praying? Am I doing it for the right reasons?

Talking about where our prayers came from is one thing. Figuring out where they go is a little trickier to discern.

As diverse as Catholic spiritual tradition is, one point that most of the great teachers come down to (and this might surprise you) is that prayer is essential for the Christian because of what prayer does for the Christian.

For example, St. Augustine said in the fourth century that we pray in order to let God shape and strengthen us for our pilgrimage of faith. As we present our lives, yearnings, and desires before God with an open heart, he corrects and strengthens us.[1]

St. Thomas Aquinas, in his exact, philosophically uncompromising way, said that we don't pray because God needs us to speak in order to know our needs, or that we need to change God. No, we pray in order to know ourselves better and to be intimately present with God.[2]

One of my favorite spiritual writers is St. Francis de Sales, who was bishop of Geneva in the seventeenth century, when Geneva was under Calvinist control. For this reason, de Sales couldn't actually live in Geneva, but he heroically ministered to his flock anyway, wrote a great deal (he's the patron saint of writers), and was a beloved spiritual director.

What distinguished St. Francis de Sales from so many other spiritual writers we find from this era is that he very consciously wrote for the laity. His great and still enormously helpful book, the *Introduction to the Devout Life,* was based on spiritual direction he gave to a French lay woman, and is dedicated to the proposition that God calls all of us to holiness, and that all of us can, indeed, be holy, no matter where or who we are. St. Francis says this about prayer: "Prayer places our intellect in the brilliance of God's light and exposes our will to the warmth of his heavenly love."[3]

Tying in with all of these reflections is the traditional Jewish sense of prayer. In English, the word *pray* means "ask," but in Hebrew, the word for pray means something else. It's derived from a word that means "judge," so that when we pray, we are placing ourselves under judgment before God, not in an aura of condemnation but of examination and purification:

> Whether we petition God to give us what we need, or thank Him for whatever good was granted, or extol Him for His awesome attributes, all prayer is intended to help make us into better human beings.[4]

This isn't any kind of modern Christian sellout to self-help thinking or humanism. The reason prayer makes us better people is this: We are God's creatures. We find our fullness, our destiny, and our truest selves in God's light, shaped and directed by his will. In prayer, we find intimacy with God and are illumined, judged, and shaped by his light, and we become whom he created us to be. It's about us, but it's about us as God's children, who will find peace only when we understand and live that way.

But what of intercessory prayer? The prayers in this book ask for many things: daily bread, help, forgiveness, and peace. What of those prayers for my kids, for my mother's soul, for my father's health, for peace, for all the suffering and the mourning throughout the world? Where do they go?

First of all, before we suggest that praying for needs is useless because God knows everything, God's in control, and God doesn't change, we have to remember one important thing: Jesus told us to pray in this way. He told us several times. He said we should ask God for whatever we need, and to do it so boldly and persistently. We should have faith, because just as a father wouldn't give his son a snake when he asked for a fish, so, too, God will "give good things to those who ask him" (Matthew 7:11).

And of course, when asked how we should pray, Jesus answered in part: Pray for daily bread and deliverance from evil. Ask.

Beyond that, we have to admit that there is great mystery. I'm no theologian, so I can really do no more than share the answers I've encountered that make sense to me.

God does not exist in isolation, nor *is* God isolation. The great mystery of God is that God is one and God is three. As theologian Luke Timothy Johnson puts it: "The trinity is the mystery of God's own life as life given and received and shared in a never-diminished abundance of being."[5]

Life on earth is a reflection of God's nature. He creates a world in which none of the parts work in isolation, in which loving community is the ground of being and action. He has created a world in which there is no useless part, no pointless dimension. All is necessary, all plays a part, including us. God could have done it another way, we can suppose, but he did not.

C. S. Lewis puts it this way:

"The efficacy of prayer is, at any rate, no *more* of a problem than the efficacy of *all* human acts. i.e., if you say, 'It is useless to pray because Providence already knows what is best and will certainly do it' then why is it not equally useless (and for the same reason) to try to alter the course of events in any way whatever?"[6]

Another writer, Bernard Bro says:

"Thus God does not change, but prayer is the means whereby he shares his plan with us. . . . in the words of St. Thomas: 'Love did not permit God to remain alone.' God is love, and love tends to share everything it has. God did not want to be alone in view of the happiness he could share and the world he could save. To us he wanted to be able to say, on the last day: You had a part in the working out of it all."[7]

We probably all have stories of prayers that have worked or been answered, as well as some questions about those we think have not. There is a great mystery here, but it rests on something solid: We are to turn to God for every need, and he will answer our prayers. This we have been promised.

What happens in the mystery of prayer is that we open ourselves to being formed by love, and that means making God's will our own. So in the end what happens is a perfect union of God's will and our lives, which not only makes the world go round, but makes the world what God always intended it to be.

Using Vocal Prayer

We know what prayer is for, and we have a sense of where it's going. Now, how do these traditional vocal prayers—or any vocal, composed prayer—fit into that?

Remember that prayer is the means by which we communicate with God and are formed by him. Any kind of prayer is "useful" to the extent that it helps us on that journey. The one form of prayer to which we are all called to participate is the sacramental life of the church, and for many of us, as well, the Liturgy of the Hours. Beyond that, the way we pray and the forms we use are totally dependent on our individual needs and personalities.

There are certainly general qualities that are common to all fruitful prayer, just as there are qualities common to any kind of good communication. No person of any time, place, or character who enters a conversation with a closed mind and a bullying mouth will be accused of having good communication skills. Similarly, if we are sincere about meeting God as he is in prayer, we need to nurture qualities of humility, charity, simplicity, generosity, patience, desire, and yes, courage.

It takes guts to pray. After all, who knows how it will change us?

Our goal is intimacy with God. What helps us get there?

The possibilities are endless: various forms of mental prayer, Scripture reading and reflection, prayer before the Blessed Sacrament, writing, drawing, sculpting, retreats, shared spontaneous prayer, liturgical prayer, and beyond.

Praying the prayers in this book, as they are or in a specific context (the rosary, the Angelus, the Liturgy of the Hours), can be helpful, too. Once again, we turn to our spiritual teachers to tell us how.

It's good to start again with Judaism, the faith that birthed ours, and the context of early Christian thinking on prayer. When Jews traditionally speak of prayer they are referring mostly to recited or sung traditional prayer, either at home or in the synagogue. A modern rabbi explains the value:

> Our sages understood the problem. They realized that few people possess the ability to express their innermost feelings and thoughts. And so they provided us with prayers composed by master liturgists and set up a formal structure within which we could give expression to the vast range of human moods, to our personal hopes and fears, to our national aspirations and experiences, to our simplest material needs, and to our highest spiritual yearnings that transcend history and reach into the infinite. They also served to teach us what to ask for and to educate us in the aspirations we should have.[1]

Jesus, along with numerous prophets of the Jewish tradition, reminded us that prayer is only true prayer when it emerges from the heart. We must always be careful, he warns us in Matthew, to attend to our motives in prayer: Don't pray so that people will see how holy you are; don't think that God is impressed by many words; pray quietly and simply.

A few centuries later, Augustine wrote that yearning is the essence of prayer and that words are not even necessary. However, because we are human, words play an important role in prayer.

When we pray with words, we clarify the content of our desire both to God and to ourselves. We are on a journey, and there is no mystery about the destination of this journey: We are pilgrims making our way to union with God, and God has revealed, through Scripture, what that means. So, if words are important to give shape to our yearnings, we would be wise not to leave that shaping up to chance or to our own untrustworthy feelings. If we entrust ourselves to the language of Scripture, especially, Augustine says, to the Psalms and the Lord's Prayer, we are letting God set the agenda for our prayer.

A millennium and a half later, Thomas Merton wrote along the same lines in his book on the Psalms, *Bread in the Wilderness*. Merton asked:

> How else had the Fathers of the Desert found their way into the regions of mystical prayer, save by the meditative recital of the Psalter? How else was the mysticism of a Gregory of

Nyssa and a Cyril of Alexandria nourished but by the Liturgy, and above all by the Psalms? . . . Contemplation will come to them when the revelation that is given, in these inspired words, to the whole Church, suddenly opens out and becomes a personal experience, a deep, transforming, mystical light that penetrates and absorbs their whole being. That light, which is the fire of the Holy Spirit, will reach them through the Psalms.[2]

Merton and St. Augustine are both emphasizing the role of the Psalms in one's spiritual life, but their words could also apply to some degree to any of our traditional prayers, shaped by time and use and treasured by the church.

Any spiritual writer you can find incorporates this kind of vocal prayer into instructions and advice. The point, of course, is never to say prayers just for the sake of saying them, thinking that there is some kind of reward in the end for merely reciting words. That kind of thinking may have crept into popular devotion, but it certainly isn't to be found in the great and lasting spiritual writers, all of whom see that sensibility as a danger, not a help in any way.

No, these vocal prayers, from the Psalms to the Lord's Prayer to Amen, can help us in the way Augustine described: they can shape our wills in the proper direction. They can also give voice to the yearnings we cannot find a way to express ourselves, and they can be quite useful when we are struggling with distractions in prayer. But whatever we do, the teachers tell us, the words should reflect our hearts.

St. Francis de Sales, for example, says that of course, anyone serious about prayer should know their Pater, Ave, and Credo in Latin and also in the vernacular. He warns the pray-er not to hurry. "A single Our Father said with feeling has greater value than many said quickly and hurriedly."[3]

St. Teresa of Ávila, a great advocate and analyst of the deepest kinds of mental prayer, makes the case for the use of vocal prayer in *The Way of Perfection*. In chapter 30 of that work, she writes that some people think that contemplation and vocal prayer have nothing to do with each other, but that is simply not true.

> [F]or I know there are many people who practise [sic] vocal prayer in the manner already described and are raised by God to the higher kind of contemplation without *having had any hand in this themselves or even* knowing how it has happened. *For this reason, daughters, I attach great importance to your saying your vocal prayers well.*[4]

Teresa goes on to describe a nun who was concerned that her prayer life was deficient because she could do nothing but depend on vocal prayer. If she failed to say her prayers, her mind wandered, so she had come back to her anchor of vocal prayer.

"She would say a number of Paternosters, corresponding to the number of times Our Lord shed His blood, and on nothing more than these and a few other prayers she would spend two or three hours."

As an old woman, this nun came to Teresa in great distress, thinking that her prayer life was less than it should be. Listening to the woman describe her inner life and seeing the holiness with which she lived, Teresa had to conclude that without even knowing it, this nun "was experiencing pure contemplation."

St. Ignatius described a prayer method centered on meditating on the words of vocal prayers, word by word. Most spiritual writers in the Catholic tradition not only have recommended this use of vocal prayers, but also recommended surrounding any other type of prayer time with vocal prayers. St. Francis de Sales said that one's hour of mental prayer should end with a Pater, an Ave, and intercessions. St. Alphonsus Liguori's method begins a meditation session with the same prayers, plus a Glory Be, and ends with the Pater, the Ave, and the Memorare.

The Franciscan St. Peter of Alcántara (1499–1562) suggested a program of mental prayer that also included the sign of the cross, the Act of Contrition, Veni Creator Spiritus, and a Psalm.

Perhaps the most accessible, most human example of the use and importance of vocal prayer is given to us by St. Thérèse of Lisieux.

Thérèse, in her spiritual autobiography, *The Story of a Soul,* admits that some forms of prayer are quite difficult for her:

> The recitation of the rosary is more difficult for me than the wearing of an instrument of penance. I feel I have said this so poorly! I force myself in vain to meditate on the mysteries of the rosary; I don't succeed in fixing my mind on them.[5]

But what does bear fruit for Thérèse, especially during difficult spiritual times, is the meditative recitation of vocal prayer:

> Sometimes when my mind is in such aridity that it is impos-
> sible to draw forth one single thought to unite me to God, I
> very slowly recite an "Our Father" and then the angelic
> salutation; then these prayers give me great delight; they
> nourish my soul much more than if I had recited them pre-
> cipitately a hundred times.[6]

So there you have it. These vocal prayers are gifts. Some will
suit us, others will not. We don't turn to them because we believe
that the words possess magic powers that multiply the more we
say them. We don't bring them back into our lives for the sake of
reviving Catholic identity or tradition for its own sake.

No, like St. Thérèse, we pray vocal prayers because, when we
offer them from the heart, they bring us into the presence of God.
Their power lies in their truth. They express truth, and they open
our eyes to truth: that God loves us; that God forgives; that we
are surrounded by people, seen and unseen, who also love and
support us; that Christ will fill us when we are hungry; that the
Spirit will embolden us when we are fearful; and that we are part
of a church, of a world, that is journeying to God.

These prayers are not mere words, because words never are.
Words always point to something else, and they always are born
of the place where there are no words. Looking at the history of
these words is one way to connect ourselves to that place as we

ourselves pray them and are mindful of the original impulse that moved someone to utter them, others to repeat them, and more to depend on them as a means to deepen their friendship with God.

As usual, someone else says it better than I can, in this case a nineteenth-century Russian Orthodox monk who was, for a time, elevated to the position of bishop, then resigned to withdraw to a monastery for twenty-eight years. Appropriately, he is named Theophan the Recluse:

> Psalms and all oral prayers were not oral at the very beginning. In their origin they were purely spiritual, and only afterwards came to be clothed in words and so assumed an oral form. But becoming oral did not deprive them of their spirituality: even now, they are oral only in their outer semblance, but in their power, they are spiritual. . . . Ponder carefully on the prayers which you have to read in your prayer book; feel them deeply, even learn them by heart. And so when you pray you will express what is already deeply felt in your heart.[7]

Glory be to the Father, and the Son, and the Holy Spirit, as it was in the beginning, is now and ever shall be. Amen.

Notes

The Journey from "You've Got a Friend" to Salve Regina

1. St. Teresa of Ávila, *Life of St. Teresa of Jesus, of The Order of Our Lady of Carmel,* 8.7.
2. St. Thérèse of Lisieux *Manuscrits autobiographiques* C 25r in *The Catechism of the Catholic Church,* 2nd ed. (Washington, D.C.: United States Catholic Conference, 1997), 614.

1. The Sign of the Cross

1. Tertullian, *De Corona,* 3
2. Cyril of Jerusalem, *Catechetical Lectures* 13.36.
3. Navarro, *Commento o Repeticion del capitulo Quando; De Conse.,* as quoted in Herbert Thurston, *Familiar Prayers: Their Origin and History* (Westminster, Md.: Newman Press, 1953), 15.
4. Evelyn Waugh, *Brideshead Revisited* (Boston: Little, Brown, 1973), 20.
5. Romano Guardini, *Sacred Signs,* http://www.ewtn.com/library/ LITURGY/SACRSIGN.TXT

2. The Our Father

1. Daniel J. Harrington, *The Gospel of Matthew,* Sacra Pagina, (Collegeville, Minn.: Michael Glazier Books, 1991), 98.
2. D. A. Carson, *Matthew,* The Expositor's Bible Commentary (Grand Rapids: Zondervan, 1984), 169.
3. Josef A. Jungmann, S.J. *The Mass of the Roman Rite: Its Origins and Development,* vol. 2, trans. Francis A. Brunner (Westminster, Md.: Christian Classics, 1986), 279-280.4.

4. St. Teresa of Ávila, *The Way of Perfection,* chap. 37, http://www.ccel.org/t/ teresa/way/chapter37.html.
5. Herbert Thurston, *Familiar Prayers: Their Origin and History* (Westminster, Md.: Newman Press, 1953), 33–35.

3. Hail Mary

1. Anthony M. Buono, *The Greatest Marian Prayers: Their History, Meaning and Usage* (New York: Alba House, 1999), 1.
2. Herbert Thurston, *Familiar Prayers: Their Origin and History* (Westminster, Md.: Newman Press, 1953), 93-97.
3. *Liber Experientiarium* in Richard Gribble, *The History and Devotion of the Rosary* (Huntington, Ind.: Our Sunday Visitor, 1992), 48.
4. Josef A. Jungmann, S. J. *The Mass of the Roman Rite: Its Origins and Development,* vol. 1, trans. Francis A. Brunner (Westminster, Md.: Christian Classics, 1986), 488.

4. Credo

1. Joseph Martos, *Doors to the Sacred* (New York: Image Books, 1982), 169.
2. Josef A. Jungmann, S.J. *The Mass of the Roman Rite: Its Origins and Development,* vol. 1, trans. Francis A. Brunner (Westminster, Md.: Christian Classics, 1986), 469.
3. Luke Timothy Johnson, *The Creed: What Christians Believe and Why It Matters* (New York: Doubleday, 2003), 64.

5. The Morning Offering

1. John L. Vessels, "History of the Apostleship of Prayer." http://www.apostleship-prayer.org/h00/h001.htm2. http://www.apostlesofprayer.org/MonthlyIntentionsGeneral.htm
2. Jean Pierre de Caussade, *The Sacrament of the Present Moment* (San Francisco: Harper & Row, 1981), 62.

6. Salve Regina

1. "Hermann of Reichenau" http://www-history.mcs.st-and.ac.uk/history/ Mathematicians/Hermann_of_Reichenau.html
2. Herbert Thurston, *Familiar Prayers: Their Origin and History* (Westminster, Md.: Newman Press, 1953), 129.

3. Ibid., 132.
4. Anthony M. Buono, *The Greatest Marian Prayers: Their History, Meaning and Usage* (New York: Alba House, 1999), 21–22.

7. The Act of Contrition

1. Josef A. Jungmann, S.J. *The Mass of the Roman Rite: Its Origins and Development,* vol. 2, trans. Francis A. Brunner (Westminster, Md.: Christian Classics, 1986), 492, n. 10.

8. The Jesus Prayer

1. Lev Gillet, *The Jesus Prayer,* (Crestwood, N. Y.: St. Vladmir's Seminary Press, 1987), 82.
2. J. D. Salinger, *Franny and Zooey* (Boston: Little, Brown and Company, 1961), 36.
3. Paul Oligny, trans., "First Life of Celano," in *St. Francis of Assisi: Writings and Early Biographies* (Chicago: Franciscan Herald Press 1972), 250.
4. Francis de Sales, *Introduction to the Devout Life,* (New York: Image Books, 1989), 99.
5. Bede Frost, *The Art of Mental Prayer,* (London: Alban Press, 1988), 62.
6. Anthony Bloom, *Living Prayer,* (Springfield, Ill.: Templegate, 1966), 85.
7. H.R.H. Princess Ileana of Romania, "Introduction to the Jesus Prayer," http://digilander.libero.it/esicasmo/ESICASM/introduction.htm.

9. Anima Christi

1. Herbert Thurston, *Familiar Prayers: Their Origin and History* (Westminster, Md.: Newman Press, 1953), 49.
2. Louis J. Puhl, S.J., *The Spiritual Exercise of St. Ignatius,* (Chicago: Loyola University Press, 1951), 32–33.

10. Angel Prayers

1. St. Augustine, *The City of God* (New York: The Modern Library, 1950), 310.
2. St. Basil of Caesaria, *Adversus Eunomium III* in *The Catechism of the Catholic Church,* 2nd ed. (Washington, D.C.: United States Catholic Conference, 1997), 87.

3. Josef A. Jungmann, S.J. *The Mass of the Roman Rite: Its Origins and Development,* vol. 2, trans. Francis A. Brunner (Westminster, Md.: Christian Classics, 1986), 456–458.

11. Prayers of St. Francis

1. Frieder Schulz, "The So-Called Prayer of St. Francis," *Greyfriars Review* 10 (1996): 242.
2. Ibid., 241.
3. Willibrord-Chrstiann van Dijk, O.F.M. Cap "A Prayer in Search of an Author," *Greyfriars Review* 10 (1996): 258.
4. Shulz, 240.
5. van Dijk, 263.
6. Paul Oligny, trans., "Legend of Perugia," in *St. Francis of Assisi: Writings and Early Biographies* (Chicago: Franciscan Herald Press 1972), 1021
7. Ibid., 1022.
8. Ibid., 1023–1024.
9. Ibid., 1076.

12. St. Patrick's Breastplate

1. Maire B. de Paor, *Patrick: The Pilgrim Apostle of Ireland* (New York: Regan Books, 1998), 131.
2. Pat Friend, "St. Patrick's Breastplate." http://allaboutirish.com/library/religion/breastplate.htm
3. A complete version, with notes, may be found at http://www.iol.ie/~santing/patrick/bplate.html

13. Memorare

1. Herbert Thurston, *Familiar Prayers: Their Origin and History* (Westminster, Md.: Newman Press, 1953), 156.
2. Ibid., 159.
3. Ibid., 156.

14. Suscipe

1. Louis J. Puhl, S.J., *The Spiritual Exercise of St. Ignatius,* (Chicago: Loyola University Press, 1951).
2. Ibid., 101.
3. Ibid., 28.

15. Veni Creator Spiritus

1. Rabanus Maurus, *Homily no. 42: On the Eclipse of the Moon,*
   http://ishi.lib.berkely.edu/history155/translations/maurus.html
2. Jungmann, II, 69, 82.

16. Grace at Meals

1. Hayim Donin *To Pray As A Jew,* (New York: Basic Books, 1980), 306.
2. Tertullian, *On Prayer,* 25. http://www.ccel.org/fathers2/ANF-03/anf03-
   51.htm#P11759_3301283
3. http://www.breviary.net/misc/grace/gracechristmas.htm
4. Maisie Ward, *Gilbert Keith Chesterton* (New York: Sheed & Ward, 1943), 61.

17. The Liturgy of the Hours

1. "General Instruction to the Liturgy of the Hours" in *The Liturgy of the Hours*
   (New York: Catholic Book Publishing Company, 1975), 21–80.
2. *A Short Breviary for Religious and the Laity.* (Collegeville, Minn.: The
   Liturgical Press, 1949), no page.
3. Ibid., no page.
4. Flannery O'Connor, *The Habit of Being: Letters,* ed. Sally Fitzgerald (New
   York: Farrar, Straus, Giroux, 1979), 159–160.
5. Kathleen Norris, *The Cloister Walk,* (New York: Riverhead Books, 1996), 92,
   100.
6. *Constitution on the Sacred Liturgy,* 4.99. http://www.vatican.va/archive/
   hist_councils/ii_vatican_council/documents/vat-ii_const_19631204_sacro
   sanctum-concilium_en.html.

18. Glory Be

1. Maxwell Staniforth, "The Martyrdom of Polycarp." In *Early Christian
   Writings* (New York: Dorset Press, 1986), 161.
2. Herbert Workman, *Persecution in the Early Church* (Oxford: Oxford
   University Press, 1980), 123–124.

19. Amen

1. Hayim Donin, *To Pray As A Jew,* (New York: Basic Books, 1980), 228.
2. Ibid., 227.
3. Justin, "First Apology" in *Early Christian Fathers* (New York: Macmillan
   Publishing, 1979), 286.

4. Cyril of Jerusalem *Catechetical Instruction 24.* http://www.ccel.org/fathers2/NPNF2-07/Npnf2-07-29.htm#P2888_823522

Where Do My Prayers Go?

1. Rebecca H. Weaver, "Prayer," in *Augustine Through the Ages: An Encyclopedia* (Grand Rapids: Wm. B. Eerdmans Publishing, 1999), 673.
2. St. Thomas Aquinas, *Light of Faith: The Compendium of Theology,* trans. Cyril Vollert (Manchester, N. H.: Sophia Institute Press, 1993), 335.
3. St. Francis de Sales, *Introduction to the Devout Life,* trans. John K. Ryan (New York: Image Books, 1989), 81.
4. Hayim Donin, *To Pray As A Jew,* (New York: Basic Books, 1980), 5.
5. Luke Timothy Johnson, *The Creed: What Christians Believe and Why It Matters* (New York: Doubleday, 2003), 251.
6. C.S. Lewis, *The Quotable Lewis,* ed. Wayne Martindale and Jerry Root (Wheaton, Ill.: Tyndale House Publishers, 1989), 484.
7. Bernard Bro, *The Rediscovery of Prayer,* trans. John Morriss, (Canfield, Ohio: Alba House Books, 1966), 15.

Using Vocal Prayer

1. Hayim Donin, *To Pray As A Jew,* (New York: Basic Books, 1980), 6.
2. Thomas Merton, *Bread in the Wilderness* (New York: New Directions, 1997), 18, 20.
3. St. Francis de Sales, *Introduction to the Devout Life,* trans. John K. Ryan (New York: Image Books, 1989), 82.
4. St. Teresa of Ávila *The Way of Perfection.* http://www.ccel.org/t/teresa/way/chapter30.html
5. St. Thérèse of Lisieux *Story of a Soul: The Autobiography of St. Thérèse of Lisieux,* trans. John Clarke (Washington, D.C.: ICS, 1997), 242.
6. Ibid., 243.
7. *The Art of Prayer,* trans. E. Kadloubovsky and E. M. Palmer, ed. Timothy Ware. (London: Faber and Faber, 1966), 56.